Edible

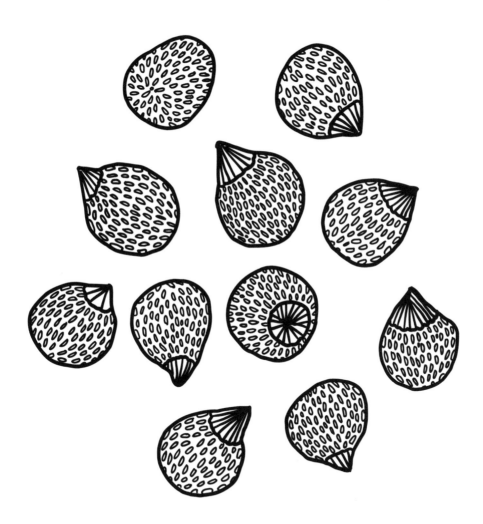

Edible

70 Sustainable Plants That Are Changing How We Eat

With over 150 illustrations

Kevin Hobbs and Artur Cisar-Erlach
Illustrated by Katie Kulla

Contents

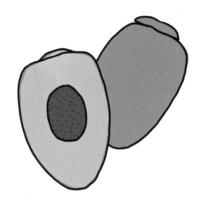

FOOD FOR A CHANGING WORLD

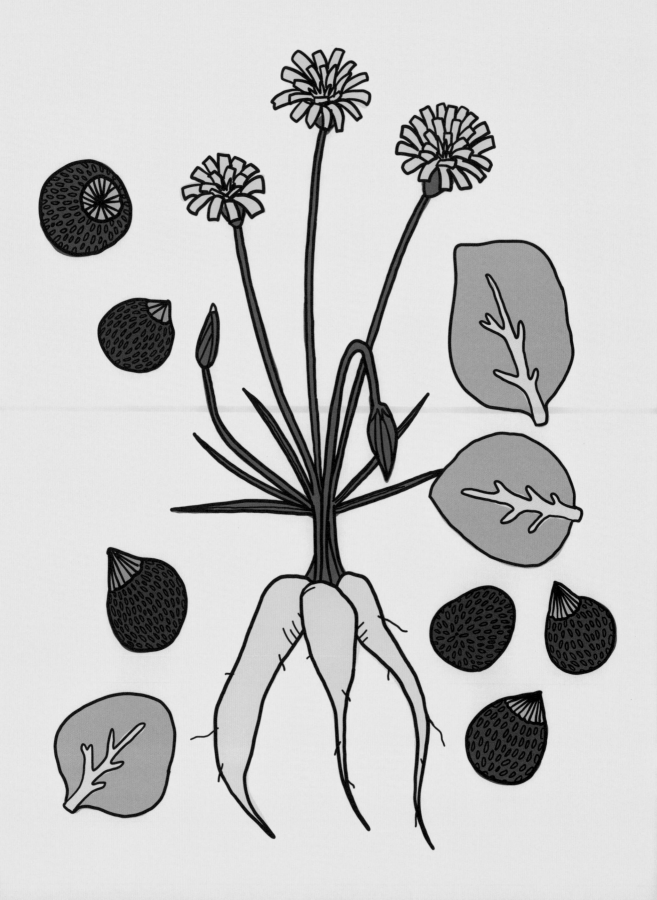

Introduction

Plants are the basis of life on Earth, providing air to breathe
and food to eat for a multitude of creatures, including humans.
They are one group of a select few that can transform sunlight
directly into food through the ingenious chemical process that
is photosynthesis. From the tiniest algae to giant redwood trees,
plants are the primary producers of the ecological pyramid.

Having had a billion years in which to adapt perfectly to the idiosyncrasies of our planet, plants are an essential part of every ecosystem. Scorching deserts and frosty mountains are as much their home as churning seas and sprawling cities. In fact, it was plants that made Earth habitable in the first place. By changing it physically and chemically, by helping in the creation of soil and by modulating the climate, they let ecosystems flourish around them, ultimately shaping Earth into the mist-shrouded blue-and-green marble it is today. It is a haven for complex life, unique in our solar system and very likely far beyond it, too.

Yet, despite the momentous importance of plants, humans take them for granted all too often, allotting them the role of decorative backdrop or even nuisance. We allow ourselves to forget about the incredible solutions they offer to the problems we face. Whether those be the countless perils of climate change, the threat of biodiversity loss or an increasingly vulnerable food system, plants are the answer.

There are in total more than 400,000 species of plant, 300,000 of which are likely to be perfectly edible. Many were consumed for millennia but simply forgotten over time, while others still play an important part in Indigenous food systems. There are many others whose broad use is feasible only thanks to recent scientific discoveries, innovative breeding techniques, and new agricultural and processing technology.

Despite all these possibilities and traditional insights into the diversity of edible plants, we have come to rely on just three for the bulk of our diet. Rice, maize and wheat are grown in ever-expanding monocultures powered by vast amounts of fuel, fertilizer and pesticide, resulting in enormous emissions of greenhouse gases. This is rapidly degrading soil, decreasing biodiversity and leaving us and our food supplies vulnerable to climate change, extreme weather, and pests and disease.

Food production, soil, water, biodiversity and climate are inextricably linked, as are the health, well-being and finances of farmers and the populations, both local and international, that they serve. Unparalleled global cooperation

is required in such disciplines as science, technology, engineering, logistics and communications if we are to come close to sustainability in the future. This is all the more challenging as discrimination, poverty, political unrest and war continue around the world. Food equality, in particular, is often beyond the control or reach of people who face apparently insurmountable hurdles, such as when and where they were born, lack of social freedom, and exposure to natural disasters and conflict.

What can humans do as individuals, then? As authors, we don't presume to have all the answers, but with this book we hope to open eyes, minds and hearts to a diversity of opportunities. What was once abstruse (intentionally or otherwise) is becoming less so in the age of digital media and increased scrutiny. But still, behind our culinary taste, curiosity and health-based preferences sits a bewildering array of sometimes conflicting benefits and costs: fair trade, support of local and/ or international economies, sustainable initiatives, the conservation of crops or traditions, against the exploitation of workers, bio-piracy, loss of habitat, degradation of soil and water, plant invasiveness and food miles. The opposing views of experts, especially on the subjects of industrial farming and genetic modification, make it even harder to form opinions.

As consumers, chefs, scientists, growers and farmers, we must all be open to change, and to changing our minds, because population growth and the onslaught of climate change will not stand still. Those of us who are fortunate enough to choose when and what we eat owe it to people in less fortunate positions to make well-informed decisions based on the best and latest information. The complacency of those with plenty may bring the experience of those with little home to roost sooner than you might imagine.

So join us on a flavourful journey of plant-based edibles from around the globe. We have found a treasure trove of fascinating specimens from six continents that thrive under the most challenging conditions. Many are already up-and-coming hardy edibles, but we have also included some that are little known outside a particular region.

We have discovered edible plants that can withstand the harshest conditions, from heat to frost and from flooding to drought. Some not only grow on the worst contaminated soils, but also clean and restore them. Some are resistant to (wild)fire, while others act as a retardant. They shake off pests and disease, thrive in swamps, filter polluted water and build soil fertility where there is none. The shade of solar panels or agroforestry systems doesn't faze them one bit, nor does the prospect of growing on an exposed roof or in a vertical farm. Some even grow in the complete weightlessness of space, while others do exceptionally well on simulated Martian soil – ensuring our future, even on other planets.

Most incredibly, though, these plants are doing all this while producing a bountiful and highly nutritious crop of fruit, seeds, leaves, flowers, bark, stems, sap and/or roots – not to mention an astonishing diversity of fantastic flavours and textures. They offer exciting new culinary possibilities for professional chefs and home cooks alike.

For us as the authors, a love of all things green and growing and the culinary delights some possess has brought new opportunities, experiences and friendships. So, visit that farmers' market, get online, and broaden your food and plant horizons by buying or growing new crops. Incorporate as many into your daily life as possible, and experience at first hand the incredible flavours they offer. Let's herald a new era of edible plants, one delicious bite at a time.

Key

You will find these icons throughout the book, indicating the characteristics of each plant according to the conditions in their native range.

 RESISTANT TO DROUGHT

 RESISTANT TO DISEASE

 GLUTEN-FREE

 ROOTS HELP TO CONTROL SOIL EROSION

 TOLERANT OF FIRE

 RESISTANT TO FROST

 RESISTANT TO HEAT

 RESISTANT TO HEAVY RAINFALL

 HIGH ENERGY FOOD SOURCE

 HIGHLY NUTRITIOUS

 CAN BE GROWN AS A LIVING FENCE

 CROP CAN BE STORED FOR A LONG TIME

 TOLERATES LOW FERTILITY SOIL

 FIXES NITROGEN IN THE SOIL

 PERENNIAL (LIVES BEYOND TWO YEARS)

 TOLERATES POLLUTED SOILS

 CROP MATURES QUICKLY

 TOLERATES SHADE

 ENHANCES SOIL QUALITY

 TOLERATES SOIL SALINITY

 TOLERATES WATERLOGGED SOIL

 RESISTANT TO WIND

 CROPS DURING WINTER

The Plants

Gurganyan

Acacia colei (Fabaceae)

Acacias are loved throughout the world. Their bright yellow (sometimes white and rarely pink), cheery, fluffy flowers brighten the short days of winter, and in warmer temperate climates they can be grown outside. The roughly 1,350 species of acacia are native to subtropical and warm temperate parts of the world, including Africa, Asia and the Americas; the Australia-Pacific region is home to the vast majority. For more than 50,000 years the First Nations people of Australia have used acacia in all aspects of life, including construction, clothing, weapons, tools and medicines.

Known as gurganyan, *Acacia colei* is a good example of intercontinental collaboration. Over the last five decades this species has been tested, developed and established as a reliable agroforestry crop in parts of Africa. Grown as a windbreak for the protection of other crops, this short, bushy tree produces clusters of bean-like seedpods that are easily harvested and processed by hand.

Perfectly adapted to the challenging conditions of arid Western Australia, the unassuming gurganyan is in fact a force to be reckoned with. It can grow in anything from nutritionally poor to very acidic, salty or alkaline soil, and its roots return nitrogen to impoverished earth. This, and the fact that its widespread root system stabilizes the soil, makes it an excellent choice for land-restoration projects. A prolific producer, the gurganyan generally bears its first highly nutritious seeds just two years after planting, and does so up to three times a year from then on.

The mature seeds can be roasted and ground into flour, which is known in Australia as wattleseed flour. A typical indigenous use is in a cake or bread baked in the coals of a fire. Other uses include pancakes, cookies, scones (or, as they are known in the United States, biscuits), granolas and even scrambled eggs. It is also used as a thickening agent in casseroles, sauces and ice cream. The seeds have a richly nutty, earthy aroma when mature, with hints of dark chocolate and roasted coffee beans, while the young green seeds have a pea-like aroma.

ALSO KNOWN AS
Candelabra wattle, soap wattle, curly-podded Cole's wattle

NATIVE RANGE
Western Australia

NATURALIZED IN
India

GROWING CONDITIONS
Thrives in subtropical and tropical regions exposed to high light levels in temperatures between 8 and 40°C (46.4–104°F), in a wide variety of soils, including red-brown stony clay, deep sand and red sandy loam. Typically prefers a neutral pH, but can be found in both alkaline and acid conditions, and tolerates marginal saline conditions. Plant in all but the wettest soils within its temperature range. A short-lived species that grows for up to ten years, it is productive from year two or three onwards. Once established, it can tolerate a light frost.

WHERE TO FIND
In food stores and speciality 'bush tucker' stores across Australia and in parts of Africa.

HOW TO EAT
Try the green seeds raw or cooked and the mature seeds (a rich source of protein) ground as flour in bread and other baked goods.

African Baobab

Adansonia digitata (Malvaceae)

ALSO KNOWN AS
Dhogwo, monkey bread tree, baobab africano, Afrikanische Affenbrotbaum, mbuyu

NATIVE RANGE
Tropical and southern Africa

NATURALIZED IN
Arabian Peninsula, many tropical and subtropical regions of Africa, and much of Asia

GROWING CONDITIONS
In varied situations, but prefers fertile, lightly acidic, sandy topsoil in seasonally wet conditions in full sun. Can withstand periods of drought, but intolerant of frost; ideal temperature range between 19 and 35°C (66–95°F). Easily grown from seed, but seedlings can take as long as twenty-three years to flower, so grafted planting stock is often used.

WHERE TO FIND
Widely available as fruit powder in health-food stores and supermarkets across the world.

HOW TO EAT
Use the refreshingly sweet and tangy fruit powder (rich in vitamin C and minerals) to make warm or cold drinks, or in smoothies, ice cream and baked goods.

To all but those living in Madagascar and northwestern Australia, who have their own baobab species, it's likely the mere mention of this iconic tree conjures up an image of the African baobab, *Adansonia digitata*. When seen against the setting sun of the sub-Saharan savanna, this prehistoric giant can't fail to elicit superlatives from visitors and locals alike. It is proven to live for at least 1,275 years, making it the world's oldest living flowering plant (angiosperm), and it is revered throughout the continent as the 'Tree of Life', for its many gifts. Peoples who live along the Zambezi River traditionally believe that baobabs were too upright and proud, a fact that angered the gods, who uprooted them, hence their upside-down appearance. Worryingly, baobab trees are dying off in greater numbers than would be expected from old age; many people believe that this represents a range shift in response to climate change, rather than an extinction event.

Essentially a giant succulent, the baobab has a vast barrel-like trunk that absorbs water during the rainy season, enabling it to produce nutrient-dense fruit (1) during the unforgiving dry season. It thrives in a wide range of poor soils and is very resistant to drought and, once mature, even fire. It stabilizes the soil, increasing fertility and the availability of water. This makes it a fascinating candidate for productive dry-land reforestation.

The self-drying fruit (2), seeds, flowers (3), young leaves and shoots are eaten both cooked and raw. Baobab fruit ranges in flavour from pear-like sweetness to a citrus-like tanginess. A typical West African recipe is a simple, creamy juice prepared by dissolving the powdered fruit in water or milk and mixing it with sugar to taste. The almond-flavoured seeds are eaten fresh, roasted, ground into a flour or paste, boiled or fermented. The slightly bitter leaves and shoots are either collected young and eaten like spinach or asparagus, respectively, or dried, ground and used in sauces, gruel or soup. The flowers, which can smell surprisingly unpleasant, are sometimes eaten raw, made into a juice or liqueur.

Grains of Paradise

Aframomum melegueta (Zingiberaceae)

ALSO KNOWN AS
Guinea pepper, Guinea grains

NATIVE RANGE
Western tropical Africa to Angola

NATURALIZED IN
French Guiana, Guyana,
Trinidad and Tobago, and
the Windward Islands

GROWING CONDITIONS
Shady forest floors in moist, rich,
slightly acid soils, tolerating some
alkalinity, in daytime temperatures
of 21–28°C (70–82°F), although
it is also found in temperatures
a few degrees either side of this
range. In colder climates, it can be
grown as a summer annual or lifted
before the first frost and replanted
when frost has passed in spring.

WHERE TO FIND
At speciality spice stores worldwide.

HOW TO EAT
Try it raw or cooked in everything
from soups and vinaigrettes to
mayonnaise, dry rubs, desserts
and even drinks.

This spice of many names is less well known outside Africa, yet it hides in plain sight as a flavouring in beers and gins. The seed of *Aframomum melegueta* – a member of the ginger family – has a unique combination of flavours: the spiciness associated with its relatives, and the texture and taste of cracked pepper. It is endemic to the tropical, swampy forests of coastal West Africa and eastwards inland, where it has been foraged and farmed for millennia as a valued cooking ingredient and to treat a plethora of ailments. Its attractive pale-pink to purple, trumpet-like flowers (1) appear at ground level, followed by yellow or red pods (2) containing reddish-brown seeds (3) – the spice. The numerous common names it has across Africa are joined by those used by traders who used the historic camel train (latterly the Silk Road), as well as those given to it by Europeans during the age of discovery.

Of the fifty or so species belonging to the genus *Aframomum*, at least fourteen are regularly traded and consumed, often from unknown sources. The name 'melegueta pepper' was universal by the fifteenth century, when Portuguese traders monopolized its source and realized the potential of this valuable spice. In an early example of rebranding, they applied the name *grãos-do-paraíso*, and 'grains of paradise' accordingly became a huge hit in Europe as a less expensive alternative to black pepper from the East. Confusion has reigned ever since between colloquial names and because of its similarity in appearance to other spices. This no doubt contributed to falling demand, and, in the case of the United Kingdom, so did increased taxes, effectively leading to its prohibition in 1825, when the government deemed its use in alcohol 'deleterious'. Meanwhile, black pepper became a household name.

Farmed production of grains of paradise is today growing to supply new demand. Unfortunately, however, this is still one of Africa's orphan crops. If ever an obscure spice deserved a bright future, it would be this one, which has the potential to improve the livelihood of countless African farmers. Being very tolerant of shade, it can be planted easily as a ground layer in existing conventional tree plantations and as part of agroforestry systems in the future. It grows rapidly, and its fragrant fruit can be harvested by farmers year after year, diversifying their income and ensuring the conservation of the species.

3

Grains of paradise seeds can be eaten both cooked and raw. As a seasoning, they are an important ingredient in West African pepper soup, in which beef, chicken, fish or goat is cooked with onions, chilli peppers, ginger, garlic, tomato puree, groundnut or peanut paste, stock (broth) and salt. Shortly before serving, the spice mix is added, consisting of calabash nutmeg, negro pepper (a local black pepper) and – the star of the dish – grains of paradise. This spice has a highly aromatic, nutty, citrusy, slightly resinous and gingery flavour reminiscent of cardamom and black pepper. Generally, grains of paradise are a great (one might even say better and more complex-tasting) substitute for black pepper.

1

2

Winged Kelp

Alaria esculenta (Alariaceae)

Kelps are marine macroalgae, 'seaweeds' that belong to the taxonomic order Laminariales, of which there are about thirty genera native to nutrient-rich, cool temperate and polar regions, where they often form vast forests. Clinging to the sea floor, they reach for sunlight to photosynthesize and, in doing so, slow down coastal erosion and sequester billions of tons of carbon dioxide every year. The need for sunlight restricts them to shallow coastal waters, where they provide habitat for a diverse array of fauna.

Although all kelp species are edible, not all are palatable, but among those that are, *Alaria esculenta* has the potential to join the world's favourite culinary seaweeds. In fact, despite being touted as 'new', it has been harvested and consumed for millennia by coastal dwellers throughout its north Atlantic Ocean range. It is often referred to as 'Atlantic wakame' for its similarity to the world's most widely consumed kelp, *Undaria pinnatifida* (wakame), of Japanese fame. Wakame has long been harvested from the wild using twined ropes, but more productive techniques have now been developed to inoculate ropes with farm-grown spores, thus safeguarding natural kelp forests. Applied to winged kelp, and combined with sustained marketing, this approach will secure its place alongside 'regular' fresh and processed vegetables in grocery stores.

A perennial cold-water specialist, winged kelp grows particularly fast in late winter and early spring, making it a great winter crop. Being grown on long lines, it offers many possibilities for open-water aquaculture, resulting in edible, highly diverse ecosystems that absorb an abundance of carbon dioxide without occupying arable land or consuming fresh water.

The blades of winged kelp can be eaten both cooked and raw. In particular, the succulent spring leaves are a favourite addition to the meat and fish broths of the Chukchi people, the Indigenous inhabitants of coastal Siberia. The midrib is crunchy, while the wings are particularly tender and therefore perfect in soups and salads. The flavour ranges from sweet, salty and nutty to an all-natural umami. Blades that are collected later in the season can be boiled, toasted or deep-fried.

ALSO KNOWN AS
Dabberlocks, badderlocks, honeyware, edible fucus, Atlantic wakame

NATIVE RANGE
North Atlantic, Bering Sea and Sea of Japan

NATURALIZED IN
Predicted either to diminish or to migrate owing to climate change

GROWING CONDITIONS
Subtidal exposed rocky shores at around 8 m (26 ft), and in exposed turbulent seas to as much as 35 m (115 ft) deep. A subject of aquaculture seaweed farming using ropes inoculated with spores.

WHERE TO FIND
At speciality stores in Europe, North America and Asia.

HOW TO EAT
Use the fresh or rehydrated blades (rich in vitamins and minerals, such as iodine) raw in salads or cooked in stir-fries and soups.

Hopniss

Apios americana (Fabaceae)

ALSO KNOWN AS
Cinnamon vine, Indian
potato, apiosu, hobbenis,
American groundnut

NATIVE RANGE
Eastern North America

NATURALIZED IN
Japan, South Korea, France,
Germany and Italy

GROWING CONDITIONS
Moist, free-draining, alkaline
to neutral soil; tolerates slightly
acid conditions. Full sun or
partial shade. Hardy to at least
-20°C (-4°F). Easily cultivated
in the ground or in containers
with plant supports to manage
its vigorous growth.

WHERE TO FIND
Tubers are mostly available
from North American
professional foragers or
adventurous home gardeners.

HOW TO EAT
Use the delicious tubers –
which are high in protein
and carbohydrates – as you
would potatoes.

Throughout recorded history, and no doubt centuries before, the tuberous roots of *Apios americana* were a staple food of the Indigenous peoples of eastern North America. Growing naturally in damp, semi-wooded areas, often alongside streams and rivers, they were traditionally foraged, and sometimes transplanted to wild areas near settlements. This was – and still is – a plant of many names, even more so once European settlers arrived and the plant was adopted by such countries as Japan. 'Groundnut', a name applied to other plants, including peanut, is often used, so it is prudent to precede it with 'American' or, even better, 'hopniss', the Unami name of the Lenape people of the northeastern United States and Canada.

A vigorous deciduous perennial vine of the legume family, hopniss can produce more than 4 metres (13 feet) of growth **(1)** as it twines round neighbouring plants or garden supports. From mid- to late summer, attractive heads of scented, reddish-brown pea-like flowers **(2)** appear. Established plants produce a mass of roots, each fine length like a string of pearls of swollen tubers **(3)** ranging in size from as small as a peanut to as large as an avocado. Commercial production has been established in Japan and South Korea, and on a small scale in the United States, but the fact that each plant can take some three years to become productive means it has limited uptake. It is seen as a viable crop for emerging agroforestry models.

This remarkable plant, adapted to a wide range of climatic conditions, not only produces a sizeable root crop that is rich in carbohydrates and protein, but also improves the soil by fixing nitrogen. Being most content when climbing vegetation at the forest's edge, it is the perfect space-maximizing addition to any temperate or subtropical agroforestry system.

The young shoots and flowers of hopniss can be eaten both cooked and raw, while its tubers and seeds must be cooked. Many Indigenous American peoples traditionally peel and boil the tubers like potatoes, or use them in hearty stews. The flavour combines the dry, starchy texture of mealy potatoes with an intriguing sweetness reminiscent of sweet potatoes, peanuts and turnips. Other delicious ways of preparing the tubers include frying, baking, drying and grinding into flour. The seeds, meanwhile, can be used in the same way as peas.

Agroforestry

Trees are one of humans' most powerful land-based allies in the fight against climate change, biodiversity loss and land degradation. Powered by sunlight, water and carbon dioxide, they already provide countless ecosystem services crucial to the functioning of planet Earth: among them sequestering and storing greenhouse gases; filtering pollutants from water and air; and cooling – the effect many of us feel most immediately in cities, towns and villages. In urban areas each tree is also a biodiversity island in itself, offering habitat to countless species.

Yet those effects pale in comparison to trees' potential in fields. When they are integrated into agricultural systems, they produce a diverse range of food products, stabilize and build up the soil, store moisture, increase biodiversity exponentially, and build agriculture's resilience to extreme weather.

This approach, called agroforestry, is the ultimate food production system of both the past and the future. It was practised in its simplest form by the earliest humans, combining fruit- or nut-producing trees with a meadow for animals to graze on, thereby multiplying the uses of a single piece of land. While trees get fertilization and animals protection from the elements, the farmer obtains tree fruit, wood and various animal products. It is also possible to combine agroforestry with field crops if trees are planted in widely spaced lines that allow regular agricultural operations to be carried out between them.

Following the multilayered structure of natural forest, an agroforestry system can be increased in complexity, for instance through the introduction of a brush layer producing edible berries, and high-canopy trees. The result is a diverse agricultural system that harnesses plant synergy and ecological processes to create productive multilayered forests that can meet all our food and material needs, while requiring much less land than conventional farming and forestry.

Much global research is currently being done into finding suitable plants for every climate, soil and agroforestry layer, and many of those can be found in this book. The idea of agroforestry can be implemented in big and small ways. Layers of fruit and nut trees, berry bushes and perennial vegetables can be planted both in large fields and in small gardens. Even pot plants can be arranged in layers, making better use of smaller spaces. So why not give the future of land-based food production a try yourself?

Following the layering principle, the top plants are those that need most light, while those in the middle should be content with partial shade and those at the bottom with full shade. A simple temperate agroforestry system could include the following plants:

TOP LAYER
Fruit trees, such as apple, cherry and pear

MIDDLE LAYER
Berry bushes, such as currant, Ebbing's silverberry and raspberry

BOTTOM LAYER
Edible perennials, such as hosta, ostrich fern and mountain spinach

Great Burdock

Arctium lappa (Asteraceae)

ALSO KNOWN AS
Gobo, ueong, Große Klette, grote klis, bardane

NATIVE RANGE
Eurasia

NATURALIZED IN
Naturalized widely in countries with a temperate climate

GROWING CONDITIONS
A lowland plant found beside streams and rivers and in other disturbed places. Tolerates a wide range of climates and grows in light to heavy, dry to moist soil in full sunshine or shade. Easily cultivated, although care should be taken to avoid escapees that can establish as weeds. This is best achieved by removing flower heads before seed set.

WHERE TO FIND
The fresh roots are available most widely in Asia, and from rare speciality growers in Europe and North America. Burdock-root herbal tea is available worldwide.

HOW TO EAT
The fresh julienned roots (a great source of fibre and antioxidants) can be braised in sweet soy sauce, used in stir-fries, soups and stews, and chipped or roasted.

From its Eurasian native range, *Arctium lappa* has, over centuries, spread slowly to become a circumpolar pioneer of temperate regions, and has amassed many local names. It colonizes disturbed areas, empty plots, parks, roadsides, fields and pasture, and some people consider it a weed, while others see it as a valuable food source to forage or domesticate. However, its use as a vegetable plant has been widely adopted. In some countries – such as Japan, where it is known as *gobo* – it is used routinely, whereas in much of Europe its use has declined since the Middle Ages. In Britain, burdock is well known as one half of the carbonated soft drink dandelion and burdock, which was developed from fifth-century recipes for the honey-based alcoholic drink mead and can now be found easily in cafes, delicatessens and supermarkets.

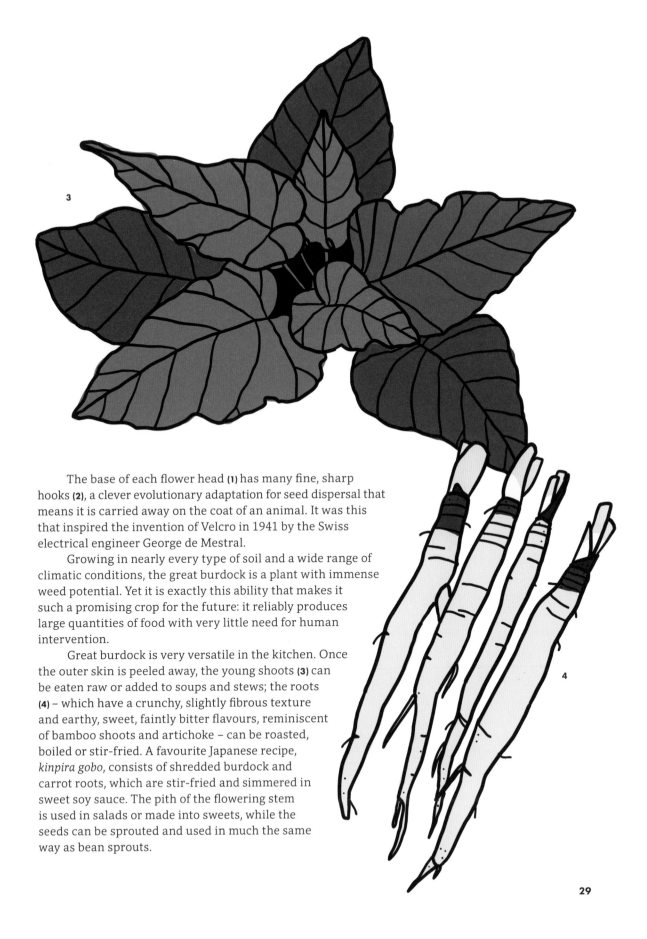

The base of each flower head **(1)** has many fine, sharp hooks **(2)**, a clever evolutionary adaptation for seed dispersal that means it is carried away on the coat of an animal. It was this that inspired the invention of Velcro in 1941 by the Swiss electrical engineer George de Mestral.

Growing in nearly every type of soil and a wide range of climatic conditions, the great burdock is a plant with immense weed potential. Yet it is exactly this ability that makes it such a promising crop for the future: it reliably produces large quantities of food with very little need for human intervention.

Great burdock is very versatile in the kitchen. Once the outer skin is peeled away, the young shoots **(3)** can be eaten raw or added to soups and stews; the roots **(4)** – which have a crunchy, slightly fibrous texture and earthy, sweet, faintly bitter flavours, reminiscent of bamboo shoots and artichoke – can be roasted, boiled or stir-fried. A favourite Japanese recipe, *kinpira gobo*, consists of shredded burdock and carrot roots, which are stir-fried and simmered in sweet soy sauce. The pith of the flowering stem is used in salads or made into sweets, while the seeds can be sprouted and used in much the same way as bean sprouts.

Breadfruit

Artocarpus altilis (Moraceae)

The mature fruit of this aptly named tropical tree in the mulberry family does indeed taste, and even feel, like freshly baked bread. It has been for thousands of years – and continues to be – a staple food of its natural and adoptive range, the Pacific Islands and beyond. This species is believed to have originated in northern New Guinea, and spread more widely around 5,000 years ago as the ancient Austronesian people of Taiwan migrated throughout the region and became known as the Polynesians. This revered plant provided not only sustenance for these early colonizers, but also wood for canoes, sap for glue, bark for the manufacture of cloth and paper, leaves for roofing and the wrapping of food, and, importantly, medicine for several ailments. More recently, in April 1789, the much-recounted mutiny on HMS *Bounty* happened while the ship was on a mission to collect more than a thousand breadfruit seedlings from Tahiti.

Artocarpus altilis has also been long established in Hawaiian culture. It declined in popularity at the end of the twentieth century but is now experiencing a resurgence in local consumption and as a lucrative and sustainable export, particularly in satisfying the market for gluten-free food.

Sometimes called the 'wonder tree', the breadfruit is remarkable indeed. Thriving in almost every condition the tropics or subtropics can throw at it, from poor, waterlogged and salty soil to windy settings, it produces an abundance of nutritious fruit only three to five years after planting, and continues to do so for decades. No wonder then that it is seen as an important part of the solution to world hunger.

The mature fruit has a texture rather like that of potato and exudes notes of freshly baked bread when it is roasted, fried, boiled or steamed; when fully ripe, it has a creamy texture and is very sweet, reminiscent of pineapple as well as delicious durian. The mature fruit must be eaten cooked, but once ripe it can also be eaten raw. For one much-loved Samoan dish, *fa'alifu 'ulu*, fire-roasted, peeled mature breadfruit is simmered briefly with a diced onion, coconut milk and salt. Breadfruit also makes a great gluten-free flour. The seeds, which taste rather like chestnuts, must be cooked and shelled before being eaten with salt, pan-fried or roasted.

ALSO KNOWN AS
Breadnut, fruta de pan, 'ulu, Brotfruchtbaum

NATIVE RANGE
Papua New Guinea

NATURALIZED IN
Widely throughout the tropics

GROWING CONDITIONS
Coastal regions of high rainfall. Easily grown in tropical and near-tropical climates in deep, fertile alluvial and limestone soil and coastal sand. Tolerates brackish waters and salt spray. Requires little intervention.

WHERE TO FIND
At markets or from speciality importers worldwide.

HOW TO EAT
Try creamy ripe breadfruit (high in complex carbohydrates) raw; the mature fruit can be roasted, fried, boiled or steamed. Use the gluten-free breadfruit flour in baking.

American Pawpaw

Asimina triloba (Annonaceae)

ALSO KNOWN AS
Pawpaw, common pawpaw, custard apple

NATIVE RANGE
Southeastern Canada, central and eastern United States

GROWING CONDITIONS
A subtropical to cool temperate small tree of the understorey of deciduous woodland and openings. Prefers deep, rich, moist acid to neutral soil. Needs full sun to fruit in abundance, but does fruit in the shade. Technically self-pollinating, but pollination increases if several are planted together.

WHERE TO FIND
Most readily available at North American farmers' markets or from experimental home gardeners.

HOW TO EAT
The delicious fresh fruit (which is high in vitamin C and minerals) can be eaten as it is or used in jams, salsas, fruit salads and ice creams.

From an ancient order of flowering plants to which the magnolias belong comes the family Annonaceae, typically of tropical distribution. However, there is one exception of note: the genus *Asimina*, which is native to temperate and subtropical eastern North America. The family expanded its range during the Miocene epoch (about 23–5.3 million years ago) as the climate heated up, ultimately receding during the cooler, drier Pliocene (5.3–2.6 million years ago) that followed. In what is probably a fluke of geographical evolution, *Asimina* was left isolated from its equatorial cousins. As a result, this curious small deciduous tree exhibits several physiological features that are common in tropical floras. Perhaps most obvious are the oversized leaves (1) with drip tips, an adaptation that sheds excess water in very humid conditions. Another is the subtle yet attractive flowers (2), which give off a faint scent of rotting meat, attracting pollinating blowflies or carrion beetles – a throwback to their ancient ancestors, which evolved before bees.

The genus is referred to collectively as pawpaw, although the prefix 'American' avoids confusion with the unrelated tropical pawpaw, *Carica papaya*. Weighing up to 500 grams (18 ounces), *Asimina triloba* is the largest fruit (technically a berry) native to North America. A rounded oblong in shape (3), it ripens from green to yellow-brown and splits open to reveal aromatic, soft, sweet yellow pulp containing two rows of seeds (4).

Being an understorey tree, pawpaws are adapted to growing in the (semi)shade, which makes them a great mid-layer addition to any agroforestry system. Furthermore, they are very resistant to disease and great at stabilizing soil.

A sizeable fruit that can be eaten both cooked and raw, the pawpaw used to be of huge importance to several Indigenous American peoples, among them the Shawnee from the Appalachian region of Ohio. It is thought to have been eaten raw, for the most part, being a convenient fast food with a creamy texture and deliciously tropical flavour reminiscent of banana and mango, with a hint of floral citrus. Today these flavours immediately supercharge a host of dishes, from jams, salsas and smoothies to muffins, ice creams, breads and puddings.

Mediterranean Saltbush

Atriplex halimus (Amaranthaceae)

ALSO KNOWN AS
Sea orache, shrubby orache, silvery orache, shrubby saltbush

NATIVE RANGE
Macaronesia, Mediterranean to western Iraq, northeastern tropical Africa and the Arabian Peninsula

NATURALIZED IN
Amsterdam and St Paul islands (Indian Ocean), Belgium, Great Britain and Iran

GROWING CONDITIONS
Saline soil is not a requisite for cultivation, since it grows on a range of free-draining soils, including pure sand. Dislikes acid soil. Most attractive and productive in full sun. Hardy to -10°C (14°F).

WHERE TO FIND
From professional foragers.

HOW TO EAT
Try the fresh leaves as a salty snack, or use as a garnish and in salads or soups. Dried leaves are a great bread herb and a low-sodium seasoning for various dishes.

Atriplex, commonly known as saltbush or orache, is a useful and fascinating genus of 247 known species of temperate and subtropical zones. Although some are found in moist conditions, many are native to dry, harsh, inhospitable inland and coastal habitats. Several species are among the most effective of all land-based halophytes, plants that grow in very salty soil or water. These adaptations evolved in the genus some 14 million years ago, during the Miocene epoch, as the planet experienced frequent drought.

Although edible, not all are tasty, but among those that are, *Atriplex halimus* is an up-and-coming one in culinary circles. It is not only tolerant of drought and salt, but also, in free-draining soil, very hardy. This, along with being perennial, makes it a sustainable crop from which fresh young growth can be harvested repeatedly, especially in otherwise unproductive arid, saline conditions. Its striking silver foliage is appealing in the garden all year round, bringing it closer to the kitchens of foragers and chefs alike.

As with many so-called new plant-based foods, this humble saltbush has been in use for millennia. Throughout its natural range, which encompasses countries of the Mediterranean, it has not only graced plates but also fed grazing livestock.

In fact, according to Jewish tradition, the leaves (known in biblical Hebrew as *maluah*) were eaten by those returning from Babylonian exile in about 352 BCE.

The Mediterranean saltbush is a true power plant. Hedgerows consisting of it can be best described as an unwavering green defensive line that not only acts as an evergreen windbreak but also stabilizes the soil while simultaneously increasing its fertility through phytoremediation (removing toxins, although this process makes it inedible). Both features are extremely valuable in a time of global desertification and soil salinization.

The glossy leaves of the Mediterranean saltbush – already referenced in the Bible (Job 30:4) as food – can be eaten raw or cooked. How it was consumed by those returning from Babylonia, one can only imagine, but if it was in the form of a salad of wild greens, the people surely appreciated the leaves' fresh, salty, slightly spicy notes. Furthermore, it can be eaten cooked, steamed or dried, and used as a condiment.

Peach Palm

Bactris gasipaes (Arecaceae)

One of the most commonly cultivated palms in South America is the peach palm, an important food for millions of people. It was already an important staple among the Indigenous pre-Columbian peoples of the Americas; early Spanish settlers in Costa Rica reported that the native Amerindians valued it so highly 'that only their wives and children were held in higher regard'. In 1575 the governor of the province of Veragua, Panama, Pedro Godínez Osorio, wrote that 'their main dish is palm grapes, which is a fruit they call *pejiballes*.' By the time the conquistadors arrived, the peach palm had been cultivated for many hundreds of years across central and tropical South America; its exact origin is therefore unknown.

A vigorous, hardy plant, the peach palm grows readily in disturbed environments and provides a nutritious bounty even in poor soils. It is considered perfect for agroforestry. It is useful as a sustainable crop for resource-poor families in Latin America and beyond, and the genetic diversity among wild and historic cultivars has allowed present-day growers to improve the fruit yield, size, flavour and ease of harvest through selective breeding. The distinctive, ferocious black spines **(1)** and the stems they adorn – which are up to 24 metres (80 feet) tall – are all but absent in their more diminutive commercial counterparts.

Called the 'palm chestnut', the fruit of the peach palm **(2)** must be boiled for several hours before they are eaten. Once cooked, the skin is peeled away and the seed inside removed. In Costa Rica, palm chestnuts are traditionally used to make a (gluten-free) flour for tortillas and a fermented alcoholic drink called *chicha*. The cooked fruit has a savoury, starchy taste that varies, with notes of cashew, chestnut, squash or potatoes.

This palm – along with some others – also provides a sought-after, edible terminal shoot known as a 'palm heart', the removal of which is fatal in single-stemmed plants. Demand for this delicacy grew to the extent that populations diminished. Today, great care is taken to harvest selectively either from multi-stemmed plants or from young plants that grow quickly and are replaced in rotation. Fresh peach palm hearts have a slightly sweet taste that is reminiscent of coconut, artichoke and sweetcorn, and are best used raw in salads, but they can also be grilled (broiled), fried, baked or sautéed. Some supermarkets offer preserved heart of palm, which can be used in the same way as fresh.

ALSO KNOWN AS
Pewa palm, pejibaye, piba, pigiguao, macana, chontaduro, pijuayo, tembe, palma de Castilla, pupunha, parepon

NATIVE RANGE
Central Bolivia north as far as northeastern Honduras

NATURALIZED IN
Widely in tropical and subtropical climates

GROWING CONDITIONS
Thrives in the lowland, humid neotropics on a variety of soils, including those that are low in nutrients. Plant in well-drained soil with moderate fertility and full sun.

WHERE TO FIND
Various fresh edible parts are available at markets throughout its growing region; preserved palm hearts are available from supermarkets worldwide.

HOW TO EAT
Enjoy the cooked fruit on its own (it is rich in minerals, vitamins and fibre) with lime or mayonnaise, or use it in a hearty soup. Heart of palm is excellent in salads or as a refreshing side dish with roasted meat or root vegetables.

2

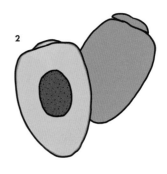

Plant Breeding and Diversity

About 12,000 years ago humankind emerged from the last ice age and took decisive steps towards the Farming Revolution. Agriculture can be placed at the heart of cultural transformation, changing the way we live and relegating the hunter-gatherer subsistence to history for all but a few peoples. From working intuitively with nature and local edible plants and animals, to trading knowledge, crops, livestock and technology, agriculture has increased food security. Inevitably, control of resources, such as land and water, along with natural and farmed crops has led to conflict, exploitation and inequality, which, despite globalization and the accumulation of knowledge, remain problematic. Life expectancy is a good illustration of this; although it is increasing, the degree by which it does so depends on where you live and, typically, the availability of nutritious food and clean water. This challenge, against a backdrop of climate change, ever-present wars and expanding global population, has galvanized the multidisciplinary approach that is essential to tackling problems of food security. Growers, environmentalists, engineers and scientists are coming together locally and internationally in the endeavour to sustain or adapt existing regional crops and develop future-proof alternatives.

Ethnobotanical knowledge of marginal or forgotten crops is therefore essential. Often already perfectly adapted to challenging conditions, such plants can provide surprisingly simple solutions to local and global challenges. From a culinary perspective they can also (re)introduce a host of fascinating textures and flavours to cuisines across the world.

For plant breeders, crops that are currently ignored are the key to introducing genetic diversity into favourite crops. Growers have always sought to improve their produce – notably flavour, size, ease of harvest and yield – through selecting seedlings or naturally occurring mutations, or as a result of targeted breeding. Yet some of these endeavours have overshot the mark, introducing diversity bottlenecks. In some cases, the best, most productive commercial hybrids have been adopted so widely that they have become victims of their own success, and the lack of genetic diversity has allowed pests and/or disease to lay waste to crops or plantations. Through harnessing biotechnology, a much-misunderstood discipline, breeders can now reintroduce the genetic diversity of forgotten edibles into many of our beloved commercial plants.

The same is true of desired traits within the same plant species. For example, one variety of a particular species might be superbly adapted to the challenges of growing at northerly latitudes, while another thrives in a Mediterranean climate. With climate change bringing Mediterranean-like conditions further north, but day-length and intensity of sunlight remaining unchanged, a combination of traits from the two varieties would be ideal. Harnessing the power of genomic research, breeders can identify the genes responsible for resilience to heat stress in the Mediterranean variety and rapidly introduce them into the northern variety using targeted traditional breeding techniques.

Another important coping strategy is the introduction of non-native food plants, particularly in regions that are suffering from extreme weather and/or soil degradation. If we are able to anticipate the alterations to growing conditions that will be caused by climatic changes, perfectly adapted plants from one part of the world can be established elsewhere, ensuring food security in the future. Great care is required not to introduce invasive species or upset local biodiversity, however.

Ultimately, a combination of all these processes and techniques will be essential if we are to introduce diversity and resilience into our food system for the future.

Desert Date

Balanites aegyptiaca var. *aegyptiaca* (Zygophyllaceae)

The Sahel is a semi-arid region of Africa that stretches between the Atlantic Ocean and the Red Sea, separating the Sahara Desert to the north and the humid savannas to the south. Since the late 1960s the region has endured a severe drought, resulting in the desertification of formerly productive land as the Sahara creeps southwards. This threat was recognized as early as the 1950s by the English biologist, botanist and environmental activist Richard St Barbe Baker, who suggested creating a 'green front' or buffer to the expanding desert. His idea was re-envisaged in the early 2000s as the 'Great Green Wall', an ambitious endeavour to plant a belt of trees 16 kilometres (10 miles) wide and 8,000 kilometres (5,000 miles) long through twenty countries. It was launched in 2007 by the African Union, and progress is being made, despite challenges and debate about the best approach.

Among the native species in this monumental reforestation *Balanites aegyptiaca*, the desert date, has been most often cited in ethnobotanical surveys as one that is desirable for its many uses. A bushy, medium-sized evergreen tree (1), it provides food, medicine, pesticide, wood fuel and fodder, and its yellow thorns were once used to pierce the skin for applying the natural black pigment used in facial tattoos. It tolerates a wide range of soils and climates, and can withstand both harsh drought and seasonal flooding. The plentiful fruit store and transport well, while the tree itself serves as an excellent living fence, windbreak and soil stabilizer.

The desert date's fruit (2), young shoots (3) and flowers can be eaten both cooked and raw, while its leaves and seeds (4) must first be cooked. The fruit has a bittersweet, astringent flavour reminiscent of gingerbread, and can be dried like dates, juiced and fermented into alcoholic drinks. It has mildly laxative properties, however, so it shouldn't be eaten in excess. A favourite Nigerian drink is prepared by boiling the fruit, known there as *aduwa*, until the pulp separates, then mixing it with lemon juice and a sweetener. The young shoots are used as a vegetable, added to soups, pastes or relishes. The sweet nectar is sucked from the flowers, or they are added to dishes during ceremonial meals. They can also be used dried, as a spice.

The seeds must be debittered through cooking before they are consumed salted, roasted, as a nut butter or ground into a protein-rich flour. They are also a great source of a cooking oil with a high smoke point. Similarly, the leaves must be cooked before they are eaten as a green vegetable.

Vine Spinach

Basella alba (Basellaceae)

Originating in tropical Asia, *Basella alba* has medicinal and culinary uses that caused it to be adopted throughout antiquity by cultures of the tropics and subtropics. The seed of this leafy green travelled ancient trade routes, along with the wisdom of India's second-millennium Sanskrit Vedas (scriptures), in which it features. Its common names – at least those that are of Western origin – typically reflect the superficial resemblance of its leaves to those of the unrelated spinach, *Spinacia oleracea*, but in fact the two are very different plants.

B. *alba* is a vigorous, heat-loving, twining perennial vine with large, fleshy, heart-shaped leaves. It can grow more than 2.5 metres (8 feet) in a season, providing an abundance of fresh leaves and growing tips. The pink-tinged white flowers, which appear in the autumn, are small yet attractive, and are followed by dark red fruit that are traditionally used in Asia as a dye and food colourant. In recent times, expats, especially those from Asia, have helped to popularize this ancient vegetable, which is now being grown by farmers and gardeners alike, often under the name Malabar spinach. Unfortunately, this name almost certainly emerged from colonial occupation, the Malabar region of western India having been exploited from the fifteenth century onwards by the Portuguese, Dutch and British.

Although regular spinach is available the world over, it is in fact difficult to grow in warm or hot regions. This is where vine spinach comes to the rescue; it thrives in heat and humidity without becoming bitter. That's a great ability to have in a time of increasing climate change-induced heatwaves.

Vine spinach can be used both cooked and raw. The delicious east Indian vegetable dish *chochhori*, which consists of various stir-fried seasonal vegetables and spices, is particularly good with chopped vine spinach leaves and shoots. Tasting similar to 'regular' spinach but with slightly peppery, citrusy notes, vine spinach is a great upgrade to any recipe that requires the standard version. Having slightly thicker leaves and a mucilaginous quality, it not only holds its consistency longer while cooking but also acts as a mild thickening agent for soups and sauces.

ALSO KNOWN AS
Ceylon spinach, Indian spinach, climbing spinach, Malabar spinach

NATIVE RANGE
Tropical Asia

NATURALIZED IN
Many tropical and subtropical regions

GROWING CONDITIONS
In scrub, forest edges, margins of cultivated land and swampy ground, and typically by rivers or streams on a range of soils. Requires full sun or dappled shade and moist, rich soil. Dry conditions and/or very poor soil induce early-season flowering, at which point the leafy growth become less palatable. Intolerant of frost, so in cold areas it should be grown as an annual or overwintered frost-free.

WHERE TO FIND
Most readily available throughout Asia and India, but offered increasingly at specialist stores in other parts of the world.

HOW TO EAT
Use in the same way as spinach.

Kochia

Bassia scoparia (Amaranthaceae)

ALSO KNOWN AS
Summer cypress, mock cypress, belvedere, burning bush, land caviar

NATIVE RANGE
Eastern Europe to temperate Asia

NATURALIZED IN
Many cool to warm temperate and subtropical areas

GROWING CONDITIONS
Can survive and thrive in a variety of soils. Tolerant of drought and salinity. In cultivation, avoid soil that is overly wet and rich.

WHERE TO FIND
Available ready to eat throughout Japan, and from speciality food retailers worldwide.

HOW TO EAT
Use the ready-to-eat seeds as a garnish to add texture to dishes.

Friend, foe, ornamental, edible or weed, depending on who you talk to and where they live – kochia is one or all of these. A medicinal herb of eastern Europe and the steppes of central Asia, this tough, resilient annual has spread throughout much of Europe, parts of Africa and, more recently, North America. The ornamental value of kochia has been celebrated throughout history, and once seen, it is never forgotten. Aided by wind, the self-pollinated, insignificant flowers (1) of late summer come and go unnoticed by all but visiting bees. What follows is awe-inspiring, especially en masse, as vivid red autumnal hues light up the landscape and inspire the alternative colloquial name 'burning bush'. As the colour fades, desiccated stems break free and tumble in the breeze, dispersing seed far and wide.

Having been introduced by immigrants to North America around the late nineteenth century, kochia became a tumbleweed of western movie fame, despite the fact that its escape to the wild was too late for its use in those films to be historically accurate. Its pioneering nature and adaptability to a range of soils and conditions, including drought, have resulted in kochia being seen by some as a pernicious weed; as such, its cultivation is prohibited in some places.

Fast-growing kochia is a highly drought-resistant force to be reckoned with. Whether a soil is saline, alkaline, contaminated with pesticides or prone to erosion, this plant will grow and slowly bring it back to health. With the thousands of tiny seeds (2) it produces, come autumn it can not only look like wildfire but also, in some parts of the world, spread like it, outcompeting staple crops, clogging harvesters and

2

resisting some of the strongest herbicides. Yet, if we can't beat it, why not eat it?

Called *tonburi* and considered a delicacy in Japan, kochia seeds can be eaten, although it is important to cook them thoroughly before carefully removing the hulls and other impurities. They are seen foremost as a garnish that gives texture to a variety of foods, from salads, udon noodles and mayonnaise to smoked fish, tofu and soy-based sauces, but can also be used as a main ingredient. With a firm, crunchy texture on the outside and a creamy, buttery consistency inside, kochia seeds have a light taste that is reminiscent of broccoli and artichoke.

1

Wax Gourd

Benincasa hispida (Cucurbitaceae)

In Southeast Asia and India, gourds are not only of nutritional and culinary importance, but also of great medicinal and cultural significance. The range of ailments treated in Ayurvedic and Chinese medicine, for example, is extensive, while gourds of many kinds are integral to a number of creation stories.

Several archaeological sites reveal the gourd's long-held importance throughout Asia, and in Thailand an example was found that is estimated to be about 9,000 years old. It is therefore not surprising that today it is considered a cultigen, a species found only in cultivation, with no known wild ancestor. This annual vine creeps or climbs quickly, using its branched tendrils to carpet the ground or, indeed, neighbouring plants. In China, it is not unusual to see it grown over bamboo frames on the banks of village ponds, suspending its fruit over the water, where it is safe from animals.

Cultivation over millennia has given rise to significant variation in the size, shape, colour and taste of the fruit, as well as the degree of waxiness or 'hairiness' that inspires many of the gourd's common names. The fruit is eaten at all stages; immature fruit are typically green, while the ripe fruit are a powdery white, and the numerous selections give attractive bluish purples.

A high-yielding annual, the wax gourd produces sizeable fruit that, thanks to its waxy coating, can be stored for many months. Being perfectly adapted to the hot lowland tropics, the plant can withstand periods of drought. It is useful for intercropping with short-duration vegetables, increasing the yield per hectare considerably. Being resistant to some soil-borne diseases, it serves as a good rootstock for several favourite cucurbits, among them melons and cucumbers.

The wax gourd's young leaves, buds, seeds and large fruit are most commonly eaten cooked. The seed can be eaten fried or roasted, in much the same way as pumpkin seeds. Immature fruit are used in a similar way to courgettes (zucchini), while mature ones feature extensively in curries, soups, drinks and pickles, or are stuffed with various fillings. Ripe gourds have a juicy texture and a mild flavour reminiscent of the white rind of a watermelon; immature fruit have a more intense flavour. The sought-after north Indian sweet known as *petha* is made by soaking cubes of wax gourd flesh in a solution of water and food-grade lime, cooking them until tender, then macerating in a sugar syrup flavoured with spices.

ALSO KNOWN AS
Bai dong gua; petha; faeng; tougan; kundru; calabaza blanca; Prügelkürbis, Chinese winter melon

NATIVE RANGE
Indo-China

NATURALIZED IN
Tropical Asia, the Caribbean, the United States and parts of Africa

GROWING CONDITIONS
Lowland tropical plant, tolerating short periods of drought on light, manure-enriched, well-drained soils.

WHERE TO FIND
Available throughout Asia and in Asian supermarkets worldwide.

HOW TO EAT
Use this mildly flavoured, high-fibre gourd as you would use pumpkins or courgettes (zucchini).

Palmyra Palm

Borassus flabellifer (Arecaceae)

ALSO KNOWN AS
Doub palm, tala or tal palm,
toddy palm, wine palm, ice apple

NATIVE RANGE
Probably western India through
Indo-China to the Nusa Tenggara
islands of Indonesia

NATURALIZED IN
Mauritania, Socotra,
south-central China, Malaysia,
Sulawesi and Thailand

GROWING CONDITIONS
In the full sun of tropical and
subtropical climates, especially
common in coastal areas. Sandy,
clay, silt or loose gravel soils of
permanent moisture, such as in
floodplains and river valleys.
Trees can live for about 100 years
and start to yield fruit after about
15 years.

WHERE TO FIND
Various edible parts are available
throughout Asia and Africa, and
increasingly in speciality food
stores worldwide.

HOW TO EAT
Try the immature seeds, known
as 'ice apples' (a rich source
of vitamins and minerals), as a
refreshing treat in hot weather.
The ripe fruit pulp is a flavourful
addition to various baked goods.

Next time you're in need of a 'hot toddy', raise a glass to India, for both the expression and the comforting blend of (usually alcoholic) spicy sweetness have their roots there. The word is derived from the Sanskrit *taldi*, the sweet, fermented sap of tal or palmyra palm on which it was originally based. *Borassus flabellifer* reaches a height of about 30 metres (98 feet) and carries a head of leaves **(1)** each as wide as 6 metres (20 feet), among which – on female trees – flowers are followed by clusters of smooth, dark brown, coconut-sized fruit **(2)**. This is a tree of great utility in tropical and subtropical climates, and as such has been traded widely throughout antiquity, a fact that obscures its true origins. Among its ancient strongholds is the southern Indian state of Tamil Nadu, where it has the honour of being state tree. Despite being celebrated in the ancient poem 'Tala Vilasam' for its '801 uses', it declined as a commodity over the twentieth century as a result of colonialism and the convenience of modern products. However, inspired by national pride and recognition of the palmyra palm's economic and cultural value, local people are seeking to bring it back to its former prominence.

Sometimes called the 'wish-fulfilling tree', the palmyra palm is truly everything one could ask for in times of global climate change. It grows across a wide range of tropical and subtropical climates and soils, handling both drought and waterlogging well. Unlike other palms, it has an extensive tap-root system that gives it a strong foothold in stormy conditions, and reduces soil erosion. It can even return arid land to fertility by storing water in its tubular roots, thereby increasing the overall availability of moisture.

The fruit and seeds **(3)** can be eaten both raw and cooked. Its inflorescence (flower head) is tapped for its sweet, caramel-like sap,

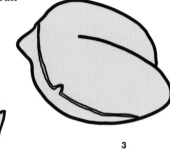

3

which can also be reduced to make palm sugar. The immature seeds have a jelly-like texture rather like that of lychee, and a refreshing flavour reminiscent of coconut. A favourite Indian dessert, *nungu payasam*, is made by adding chopped immature palm seeds to reduced milk flavoured with cardamom and saffron.

The ripe fruit pulp is similar to baked pumpkin and can be used in jams or jellies, juices, and baked and steamed goods. The sprouted seeds have a crisp consistency and a strong flavour rather like that of the sap.

1

2

Safflower

Carthamus tinctorius (Asteraceae)

Known, rather negatively, as false saffron, the safflower has petals **(1)** that bear a close resemblance to the prized threads (stigma) of saffron. Both safflower and saffron bring colour to food, but there ends the similarity.

Safflower is a multipurpose plant, with edible oil, seeds and thistle-like leaves **(2)**, and it can be used medicinally and as a natural dye. This, together with its general robustness, has meant that it has been in continuous cultivation for more than 5,000 years, and there is increasing awareness of its potential. Evidence points to safflower originating in ancient Mesopotamia, a region that today encompasses Turkey, Syria and the eastern Mediterranean.

As a highly resilient annual, safflower can thrive in nutritionally poor, alkaline or salty soils. Neither frost nor drought can keep it from reliably producing flowers and seeds, which are the basis for a nutritious oil, rich in essential unsaturated fatty acids. Originating on windswept plains, it is well equipped for the environmental challenges of our time, and promises to become one of the most important oilseed crops for the rapidly expanding arid and semi-arid regions of the planet.

Safflower shoots, flowers and young leaves are edible both cooked and raw. The seeds are mostly consumed as an oil, but can also be eaten raw, toasted or turned into a plant-based milk. A simple and delicious Indian rice pudding, *kusubi huggi*, is made by soaking, blending and straining safflower seeds to create a milk that is then simmered with cooked rice and salt. Raw safflower seeds and their milk have a nutty, slightly bitter taste, while the oil has a very mild, almost neutral aroma. That and its very high smoking point make it useful for roasting, frying and baking.

The slightly bitter young shoots and leaves are used in salads and stir-fries, as a pot herb and in teas. Safflower petals **(3)**, meanwhile, are used in a wide variety of dishes, mostly for their colouring properties but also for their lightly floral, chocolatey, sweet aroma.

ALSO KNOWN AS
Dyer's saffron, false saffron

NATIVE RANGE
Central and eastern Turkey to Iran

NATURALIZED IN
Widely in suitable climates

GROWING CONDITIONS
Grows in a range of poor, dry soils in the semi-arid subtropics. Adapted to high temperatures and bright light, making it tolerant of long periods of drought as well as high winds and periods of heavy rain or hail. Plant in uncultivated or lightly cultivated dry soil with low to moderate nutrients. Grows best between 20 and 32°C (68–90°F), although it will tolerate slightly lower and higher temperatures.

WHERE TO FIND
Seeds, oil and flowers are available in food stores throughout the eastern Mediterranean, Asia, the Americas and eastern Europe.

HOW TO EAT
Safflower is a great source of vitamin E. Try the leaves and shoots in salads, stir-fries and teas. Use the petals to colour dishes in the same way as saffron.

3

Sea Grapes

Caulerpa lentillifera (Caulerpaceae)

ALSO KNOWN AS
Bulung, green caviar, bigas-bigasan, arosep, umi-budō, latô

NATIVE RANGE
Coastal Indo-Pacific

GROWING CONDITIONS
Tropical coastal calm waters of shallow, sandy to muddy lagoons that are not exposed at low tide. Cultivated in farmed ponds at a depth of around 1 m (3 ft) or inland in seawater pools that mimic marine conditions.

WHERE TO FIND
Available fresh throughout the coastal Indo-Pacific, and globally in dehydrated form from specialized online retailers.

HOW TO EAT
Sea grapes are high in unsaturated fatty acids and antioxidants. Enjoy them as a tasty salad, or use as an attractive garnish for stir-fries, soups and rice dishes.

Most palaeoanthropologists agree that the oceans' edible bounty played a major role in the evolution of *Homo sapiens*, in more ways than one might imagine. A shore-based diet, including nutrient-rich seaweeds, helped humans to grow bigger brains, but many believe that this also helped them to avoid extinction. During the Penultimate Glacial Period (about 194,000–135,000 years ago), it is thought that the southern coast of Africa provided a safe haven for humans, where they could eat migrating mammals and an abundance of shellfish, marine life and edible plants. So began humankind's use of seaweed as a food for both themselves and their livestock. Historically, many of the world's coastal populations have harvested marine algae, but over the millennia land-farmed crops have all but replaced them. The exception is some countries in East Asia, where seaweed has been an ever-present item on the menu. Among the favourites are sea grapes or *latô*, the Filipino name for *Caulerpa lentillifera*, which resemble numerous bunches of very tiny green grapes – or indeed caviar, as some local names suggest. Traditionally harvested from the wild, the plant was first cultivated commercially in the 1950s in the Philippines province of Cebu, since joined by such countries as China, Japan and Korea.

With 71 per cent of the Earth's surface consisting of ocean and the remaining 29 per cent of land that faces increasing pressure, sustainable sea-based food production is a hugely important pillar of global food security. Sea grapes are an excellent example of how sea vegetables can be a significant food resource, being already one of the most economically important edible algae in the world. Especially when integrated into a polyculture system, open-water farms can create a sustainable livelihood for many coastal communities, while protecting the environment, conserving biodiversity and absorbing copious amounts of carbon dioxide.

Sea grapes are eaten either raw, or dried and rehydrated. Often described as 'tasting like the ocean', they have a pleasurable pop when bitten into, and briny, slightly sweet-umami flavours. They are used in soups, stir-fries and rice, dipped into soy sauce or even incorporated into ice cream. A popular salad in the Philippines consists of sea grapes, diced tomatoes and onions, all marinated with a dash of vinegar, fish sauce and fish paste. As with any seaweed, it is advisable to consume sea grapes in moderation to avoid eating too much salt, iodine and heavy metals.

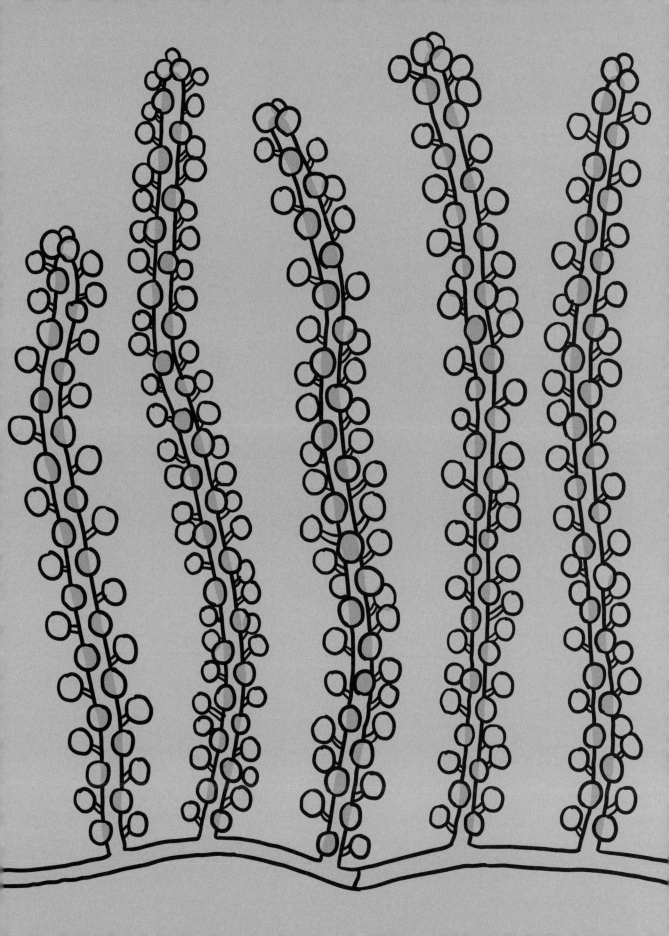

Foraging

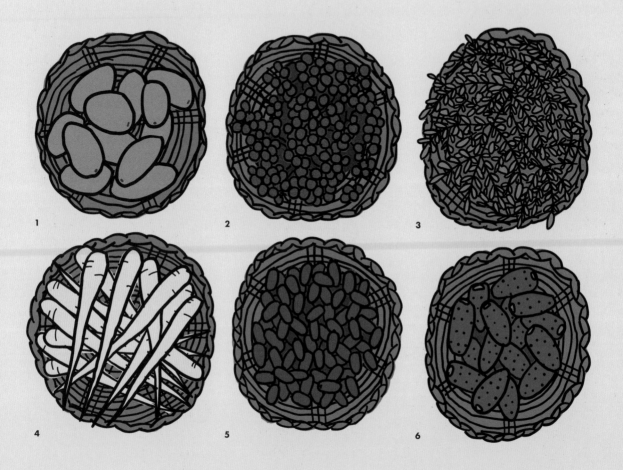

For most of human history, hunting and gathering wild food was the way of life. It sustained our ancestors and allowed them to build complex societies. While many had to stay on the move, at least seasonally, to find enough to eat, some managed to settle, living off bountiful wild resources.

All this changed with the advent of agriculture, and nearly all societies became more sedentary, focusing their efforts on a few highly productive crops and animals. Today only a very few hunter-gathering groups remain.

Yet foraging – gathering wild food – still contributes to subsistence in many parts of the world. In recent years it has gained considerably in popularity as more and more people have discovered it as a pastime. It is a great way of connecting with the environment, learning to identify various wild plants, and introducing exciting new flavours and textures into the kitchen. If done responsibly, it is also a great way of diversifying the diet and supplementing it with healthy ingredients that can't be found in any supermarket.

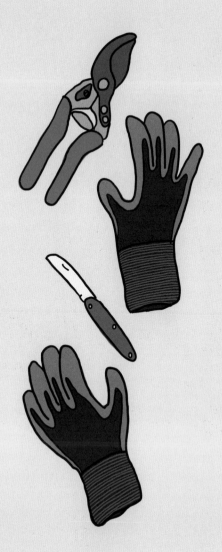

When trying foraging yourself, it is important to follow a few simple rules:

I. Make sure that foraging is allowed in general in your area, and that you have asked permission of the landowner.

2. Always be certain that you have identified the plant correctly. This is particularly important for mushrooms.

3. Know which parts are edible at which time of the year, and how to prepare them safely.

4. Never over-harvest, and keep in mind that the plant will be a crucial resource for many wild animals.

5. Collect plants only where they are growing in abundance.

6. Harvest carefully, causing as little damage as possible.

7. Steer clear of protected areas and species.

8. Avoid polluted areas, such as the sides of busy roads.

For inspiration, and to find out which plants can be foraged in your area, see page 197. Many can also be grown in the garden or in pots.

Plumed Cockscomb

Celosia argentea (Amaranthaceae)

Food, weed, bedding or house plant, even spiritual offering: *Celosia argentea* is considered one or all of these to people throughout the world. But all would agree on its natural (or, in most cases, cultivated) beauty. It is immediately recognizable for its flame-like inflorescences, reminiscent of a colourful cockscomb. Outside its native and naturalized home of pantropical regions, it is seen purely as a colourful annual bedding plant, but to many people it is much more. It has been and continues to be used to treat many ailments as part of systems of traditional medicine. In southern Nigeria it is known as *soko yokoto*, which translates as 'the vegetable that makes your husband's face rosy'.

The plumed cockscomb has mystical and religious significance for some people, and is often used as an offering or planted in temple and domestic gardens. Today seeds and plants are readily available, and breeding has added to the diversity of flower colour and form for the garden and cut-flower market, including those that resemble coral or, to some, a brain. Many of today's cultivars have been bred for beauty, but increasing attention is now focused on varieties that taste good and crop well.

Although it is considered an obnoxious weed in some parts of the world, in West Africa the plumed cockscomb is a sought-after leafy vegetable. It grows very fast in a wide range of soils, resisting high temperatures and short periods of drought, and producing a bountiful crop of nutritious greens. Its leaves, young stems and flowers are therefore of particular importance in Nigeria, where they are eaten raw or cooked. A traditional stew, called *èfó riro* in Yoruban, consists of a rich pepper sauce, a selection of fresh and smoked fish, various meats, *irú* (fermented locust-bean paste) and chopped leaves of the plumed cockscomb. The green is also incorporated in soups, sauces and porridge, or steamed and eaten as a side dish, much like spinach. Indeed, its texture and flavour have many parallels to spinach, although it is slightly more bitter.

ALSO KNOWN AS
Lagos spinach, soko yokoto, qing xiang, borlón, Silber-Brandschopf

NATIVE RANGE
Believed to have originated in tropical Africa

NATURALIZED IN
Has become a pantropical weed

GROWING CONDITIONS
Sun or partial shade in humid tropical and subtropical climates, on riverbanks, floodplains and grassland. Does best on moist but free-draining soils. Adapted to hot and humid climates, and less susceptible than many other crops to fungal infection, such as mildew. Easily grown as a summer annual in cooler temperate climates.

WHERE TO FIND
At markets throughout West Africa and Southeast Asia, and worldwide as an edible ornamental plant.

HOW TO EAT
The tasty leaves are high in protein and antioxidants, and can be used in the same way as spinach.

Carob

Ceratonia siliqua (Fabaceae)

ALSO KNOWN AS
St John's bread, locust bean, al-kharoubah, caroubier, Johannisbrotbaum

NATIVE RANGE
Believed to be native to the Middle East and coastal northeastern Africa

NATURALIZED IN
Widely in suitable climates

GROWING CONDITIONS
Naturally occurring in a wide range of poor, dry, typically free-draining soils in exposed or semi-sheltered situations, where it can encounter temperatures ranging from -4 to over 40°C (25–104°F). In cultivation, prefers sandy, well-drained loam.

WHERE TO FIND
Supermarkets and health-food stores worldwide.

HOW TO EAT
Use carob powder – which is high in fibre – in the preparation of sweet warm drinks (such as hot chocolate) and for gluten-free baking.

This handsome evergreen tree flowers (1) in the autumn, after which it produces large, bean-like pods (2) characteristic of the legume family, to which it belongs. Throughout the carob's historic range of the Middle East and the Mediterranean, few other trees have been written about so often and with such reverence. Among religious texts, the Mesopotamian *Epic of Gilgamesh* from about 1800 BCE is the first to record the carob tree, and the story it offers of Enkidu and Shamhat is widely acknowledged by scholars to be the inspiration for the much later narrative of Adam and Eve. The word 'carob' is derived from the Arabic *kharrūb*, 'locust bean pod', and it is likely that this was the 'locusts and wild honey' of the New Testament that allowed St John the Baptist to survive the desert. The Jewish Talmud and the Koran of Islam also feature this incredible tree, a fact that is testament to its historic importance. The uniform size and weight of its seeds (3) meant that they were used in ancient times in valuing gold and gemstones as *qirat*, Arabic for 'fruit of the carob', from which comes the word 'carat'. The Romans' pure gold coin, the *solidus*, weighed twenty-four *qirat* and so became the measure of gold's purity.

Not only growing in extreme drought and heat, but also thriving and fruiting when all other crops fail, the carob tree has long been considered miraculous. It does indeed have many extraordinary abilities. Whether in alkaline, salty, nutritionally poor or dry, rocky soil, it will not only make its home but also swiftly improve it with its deep-reaching, solidifying roots and by fixing atmospheric nitrogen. It is an ideal and highly productive windbreak for any dry-land system of agroforestry.

The pulp in the carob's seedpods can be eaten both raw and cooked, while the seeds can be milled into flour, roasted for a caffeine-free

3

coffee substitute, or made into an edible gum. An extremely delicious and versatile Lebanese sweetener, *dibs el kharrub*, is made by cooking carob pods in water, then reducing the liquid to a syrupy consistency. The dried seedpods taste rather like chocolate, making it a great substitute. The seeds can be made into a gluten-free flour, while locust-bean gum is used widely as a thickener and gelling agent.

1

2

Irish Moss

Chondrus crispus (Gigartinaceae)

Land plants were born of freshwater green algae some 500 million years ago, leaving their red counterparts behind to evolve into the oceans' diverse seaweeds. Since red light struggles to penetrate water, red seaweeds (which are not all actually red) adapted to harvest energy from blue light, the last colour to disappear in the twilight of deep water. Of them, *Chondrus crispus* is one of the most commonly consumed. Even if you've never heard of it, you have almost certainly eaten it; the food additive carrageenan is often produced from Irish moss and is used to thicken, emulsify and preserve myriad foods including cottage cheese, ice cream and many alternatives to dairy. However, scientists are now debating whether it has implications for human health. So, it's important to note that carrageenan is a chemically processed form separate from the nutritious wholefood Irish moss, which has a long culinary history. The name 'Irish moss' reflects a long history of use and abundant growth in Ireland, where it was a vital food during the Great Famine in the mid-nineteenth century.

Since Irish moss clings steadfastly to rocks underwater and also thrives in free-floating form, it is a prime candidate for both open-water and tank aquaculture. It is moderately tolerant of heat, so can both withstand the effects of climate change and actively remedy it through carbon fixation.

The fronds can be eaten both raw and cooked, and the preparation most commonly made from them is Irish sea moss gel. To make it, the raw, dried leaves are soaked in water overnight, rinsed, then blended with a new batch of cold water until smooth. This highly nutritious gel with a flavour reminiscent of iodine, seaweed and oysters can be added to smoothies, soups, sauces and desserts, and works as a natural, vegan, gluten-free thickening agent. Commercially produced powders and gels offer a flavourless alternative. The high iodine content means it is advisable to consume it in moderation, however.

ALSO KNOWN AS
Jelly moss, carrageen moss

NATIVE RANGE
Atlantic coast of Europe and North America

NATURALIZED IN
Range is predicted to shift with climate change

GROWING CONDITIONS
On rocks and in tidal pools. Most abundant 4–7 m (13–23 ft) below average low water. Successfully farmed in open-water and tank aquaculture.

WHERE TO FIND
Dried fronds, flakes, powders and gels are available in health-food stores worldwide.

HOW TO EAT
Use fresh or rehydrated to make the vitamin- and mineral-rich Irish sea moss gel, for use in smoothies, soups and sauces.

Coffee Cherry

Coffea arabica and *C. canephora* (Rubiaceae)

ALSO KNOWN AS
Cascara, coffee berry

NATIVE RANGE
C. arabica: Ethiopia, Kenya
and Sudan
C. canephora: Western tropical
Africa to South Sudan and
northern Angola

NATURALIZED IN
Widely in suitable climates

GROWING CONDITIONS
Tropical climate, humid evergreen
forests, preferring cooler, higher
elevations on rich, slightly acidic
humus soils. Can be cultivated
outdoors or under glass if natural
conditions are maintained. Avoid
drying winds and temperatures
lower than 5°C (40°F).

WHERE TO FIND
The fresh fruit is available only
in coffee-growing regions,
but the dried fruit (*cascara*)
can be ordered from speciality
retailers worldwide.

HOW TO EAT
Coffee cherries are high in
antioxidants. The fresh fruit are
great for jellies, jams or juices;
use the dried *cascara* to brew hot
or cold tea that is low in caffeine.

From a small tree of Ethiopia's mountain forests, coffee has become one of the world's most economically important plant-based products. It's now so widely enjoyed that we forget – or don't realize – that it's relatively new, having been first consumed in the mid-fifteenth century. The Yemenis were the first to grow and enjoy coffee outside its homeland, having boiled *Coffea* beans, the seed, to produce *gahwa*, 'that which prevents sleep'. The Sufi, Muslim mystics, are believed to have first harnessed coffee's stimulating properties, to bring focus and clarity to their nightly prayers. Despite concerns about its effect on morals, it swept through the Arabian Peninsula and beyond, and of course the rest is history.

But what of the fruit, known to many as coffee cherry, that surrounds the bean belonging to the two species of international trade? It too was, and still is, used in a drink, but one more akin to fruit tea, containing only about a quarter of the caffeine of the more familiar brew. Familiar to present-day coffee-house connoisseurs, drinks flavoured with coffee cherries are on the rise, and at times the raw ingredient is more valuable than the beans. This is excellent news for growers who have, beyond local demand, generally considered the fruit waste material, good only for use as compost. Typically ripening bright red (1), the fruit, once removed from the bean (2), is dried to a golden brown and sold as *cascara*.

Although it is already used extensively in agroforestry systems, coffee has much more to give. It offers an excellent lesson against the single-minded use of crop plants that is so common today. What is habitually labelled 'waste' or 'by-product' is often a missed opportunity for the sustainable use of the planet's increasingly limited resources. Such materials are frequently given away for

2

free, offering many exciting, truly impactful opportunities for creative entrepreneurs.

In both texture and flavour the fruit of the coffee bush resembles the cornelian cherry (see page 64), but less astringent; it can be eaten fresh or used in jellies, jams, juices, drinks and sauces. In Ethiopia, *buna keshir* is made from the roasted cherries and drunk in water or milk flavoured with honey or salt, while *qishr*, of Arab origin, is sugared and spiced with ginger or sometimes cinnamon. The toasted leaves make an excellent tea, called *kuti* in Ethiopia, with a delicate, nutty flavour reminiscent of some green teas.

Cornelian Cherry

Cornus mas (Cornaceae)

The cornelian cherry has a long and fascinating history throughout its native and historically expanded range of western Europe eastwards. It is popular today as a tough, hardy ornamental with small but cheery golden-yellow flowers that brighten the leafless stems of late winter. The summer fruit are roughly the size and shape of olives but rich red – carnelian – in colour, reminiscent of cherries, to which they are unrelated. The flavour can be described as sour-sweet, the latter prevailing in fully ripe fruit, especially of those varieties that have been selected for eating straight from the bush.

Throughout antiquity the fruit of *Cornus mas* has been used in medicine, eaten fresh and processed into food and drinks, so it is well documented from early times. It features in the epic poem the *Odyssey* (about 725–675 BCE), attributed to the Greek writer Homer. In Serbia an old saying persists, *'Zdrav kao dren'*, 'as healthy as a cornel', in reference to the fruit's health-giving properties. The hard, durable wood has long been used in the making of tools and wheel spokes, and was the material of choice for a range of ancient weapons.

Having featured extensively in Europe's original agroforestry system – the diverse hedges that were used as field boundaries by Celtic peoples – the cornelian cherry is increasingly making a comeback across the continent. Growing across a good range of soils and climates, it is particularly frost-hardy. This makes it a useful, highly productive choice for windbreaks and shelter belts in northern latitudes. It is a great food resource for pollinators in the spring, being one of the earliest plants to bloom, and also for birds in the autumn.

The fruit is edible both raw and cooked, and features in many central and eastern European recipes. It can be made into sweet chutneys, syrups and juices, and even brined or preserved in oil, much like olives. The fully ripe fruit has a texture similar to harder cherries and a flavour reminiscent of sour cherries and cranberries. A typical Austrian preserve, *Dirndlmarmelade*, is made from it, and pairs well with everything from pancakes and bread to chocolate cake and ice cream.

Tiger Nut

Cyperus esculentus (Cyperaceae)

In what should be considered a renaissance, the nutritious dried tubers, tiger nuts, of *Cyperus esculenta* are finding their way into the aisles of health-food stores as the latest 'superfood'.

However, as is often the case, they have a long history as such. In fact, scientists believe they were enjoyed by humans' distant cousins, *Paranthropus boisei*, as far back as 2.3 million years ago. Tiger nuts would have been beneficial to the developing hominid brain, since they contain relatively large amounts of minerals, vitamins and fatty acids. They have been cultivated for millennia, and evidence of their more 'recent' importance has been found in the form of dry tubers in the 6,000-year-old tombs of predynastic Egypt. The ancient Egyptians enjoyed them roasted and used them as a sweetmeat, a pleasure they insisted on for the afterlife, along with dates, figs and other foods.

In southern Europe the tiger nut has been cultivated for many centuries. The ancient Greek botanist Theophrastus wrote about boiled, sweet tiger nuts in his *Historia Plantarum* in the third century BCE, while in thirteenth-century Spain they were being used as an ingredient in the sweet drink *horchata de chufa*.

Considered by most to have originated in Europe, Asia and Africa, the tiger nut is now found in almost all temperate, tropical and subtropical regions of the world, and is regarded as a pernicious weed by many farmers. Yet it is exactly this 'superweed' potential that makes it such a powerful food ally. Growing vigorously in every type of soil from compacted and waterlogged to dry and sandy, it can decrease wind erosion in barren land and improves the quality of soil overall – all while producing a bounty of highly nutritious tubers.

The tubers can be eaten cooked or raw, or dried and ground into a powder. Tasting like a sweet cross between pecan and Brazil nuts, they are rather chewy so are better eaten processed; they can be made into everything from nut butters and smoothies to salads, ice creams and baked goods. Much like its thirteenth-century predecessor, today's *horchata* is made from soaked, ground tiger nuts mixed with sugar, cinnamon, vanilla and ice. Tiger nuts are also the source of a desirable cooking oil, with a rich, nutty taste and a very high smoke point.

ALSO KNOWN AS
Yóu suō cǎo, earth almond, yellow nut sedge, Erdmandel, amande de terre

NATIVE RANGE
Believed to have originated in Europe, Asia and Africa.

NATURALIZED IN
Widely in suitable climates

GROWING CONDITIONS
Favours muddy soil and shallow water; also grows as a weed of cultivated ground in everything from acid black peat to lightly alkaline soil. Thrives in warm climates and hot tropical climates. Can be grown in containers.

WHERE TO FIND
At speciality and health-food stores worldwide.

HOW TO EAT
Try processed tiger nuts (which are rich in fibre and essential fatty acids) as nut butter, and in smoothies, drinks and ice cream. Use the gluten-free tiger-nut powder in baking.

Fonio Millet

Digitaria exilis (Poaceae)

ALSO KNOWN AS
Kang, acha, figm, kafea,
hungry rice, digitaria

NATIVE RANGE
Western tropical Africa
to Cameroon

NATURALIZED IN
Dominican Republic, Haiti
and Guinea-Bissau

GROWING CONDITIONS
An easily grown annual grass
of sparse woodland and
grassland on a range of dry to
moist soils in tropical climates.
The various landraces take
between eight and twenty-five
weeks from planted seedling
to harvest.

WHERE TO FIND
Increasingly available worldwide
from West African speciality
food stores.

HOW TO EAT
Rich in vitamin B and minerals,
fonio millet can be used much
like quinoa.

In the race to create high-yield, low-input cereal varieties to suit mechanized farming systems, most present-day crops have been subject to intensive breeding and, in some cases, genetic modification. More attention is now being focused on what are regarded as 'ancient grains', and their adaptability to specific growing conditions. Although there is no strict definition of an ancient grain, it is widely considered to be one that, over time, has remained largely unchanged beyond natural or semi-natural landraces (locally adapted varieties) that have emerged in response to changing climate and conditions. Such grains as bulgur, einkorn, emmer, amaranth and quinoa are increasingly popular, and, as with wholegrains more generally, are more healthy than refined varieties.

A rising star among ancient grains is fonio, promoted by many as 'the world's tastiest cereal'. A knee- or waist-high grass of dry West African savannas, it was first gathered some 5,000 years ago, and later cultivated. Archaeological evidence, including that of ancient Egyptian burial grounds, reveals its place among the continent's earliest cultivated crops. During the nineteenth century the popularity of fonio began to dwindle as newer grains were introduced that were perceived as superior and certainly easier to process, if they reached harvest. Today fonio production is growing to meet demand locally and internationally, in recognition of this 'miracle' grain's flavour and nutritional value.

Fonio millet's natural ability to grow in poor, sandy soil, including that degraded by unsustainable farming practices and climate change, makes it a contender to help with future food security in countries and regions facing these challenges. Its extensive root system reaches deep soil moisture and helps to prevent soil erosion. It grows rapidly, with very little human intervention, but the harvesting and processing of this tiny grain are still a challenge. Fortunately, a drive for the design of bespoke

machinery is well underway, and should finally surmount this last hurdle to wider adoption.

Fonio has a texture similar to couscous and a deliciously nutty flavour that lends itself to a host of dishes, from stews and salads to pilafs and baked goods. The grains can be eaten cooked, in much the same way as quinoa, or ground into flour. For a favourite northern Nigerian dish, *pate acha*, grated garden eggs (a small, bitter aubergine/eggplant), hot peppers, onions, carrots, spinach, sour sorrel leaves and fonio are added to beef-bone broth, resulting in a savoury porridge.

The Future of Bread

What would the world be without bread? From Polish bagels, Chinese *shaobing*, Italian ciabatta, Egyptian *aish baladi*, German pumpernickel, Icelandic *dökkt rúgbrauð* and French baguette to Ethiopian *injera*, British crumpets, Indian paratha and Chilean *pan de huevo*, for most of us it is hard to imagine going a day without at least one chunk of bread.

Bread even pre-dates the Farming Revolution, being already consumed 14,000 years ago by the Natufians, a people of hunter-gatherers living in what is now Jordan. Who knows, maybe it was the prospect of an endless supply of delicious bread that motivated our ancestors to go all-in on grain-based agriculture in the first place. Whatever the reason, cereals are today the world's main crop, clocking in at nearly 3 billion tons per year or almost one third of everything that's grown. While more than half of that is used as animal feed or for industrial processes, such as making biofuel, cereals still constitute the major part of the world's dietary energy supply, and much of this is consumed in the form of bread and other baked goods.

Yet cereals are by ecological definition pioneer species, meaning that they are one of the first plants to colonize barren environments: recently flooded river plains, wildfire-ravaged ecosystems, landslide areas or even newly arisen islands. This makes them a fantastic, high-yielding crop for marginal, naturally disturbed land or under drought conditions. Growing cereals in more productive environments means resetting the ecological clock every year to zero – barren earth – to re-create the optimal growing conditions. This not only requires enormous amounts of energy, typically derived from fossil fuels, but also continuously degrades the soil by not allowing it to accumulate fertility naturally over time, leading eventually to a need for even more energy in the form of fertilizer.

This is a vicious cycle that has resulted in a great deal of degraded land across the world. To prevent this from happening further still, productive environments must be used for more ecologically complex, perennial agricultural systems, such as agroforestry, which naturally build up soil fertility over time without needing excessive amounts of energy. Cereals can be integrated into those systems, perhaps by being sown between lines of productive trees, but in a way that gives them a less dominant role.

Growing less cereal doesn't mean we must abstain from our beloved daily bread, however. On the contrary: bread is in the middle of an exciting, cereal-free transformation that was started inadvertently by the gluten-free movement. Suddenly numerous home and professional bakers are developing ever more delicious recipes, taking advantage of the incredible number of plants that can be used to make flour: green bananas, acorns, cacti paddles, potatoes, breadfruit, hopniss, peach palm and many more. Bread already boasts a huge variety of gluten-free textures and flavours, and this development points towards an exciting future centred on an incredible diversity of plant resources. Such diversity is at the heart of a resilient and sustainable food system.

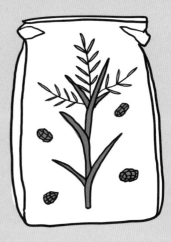

If you want to experience the future of bread today, try incorporating the following into your baking:

- **ACORN FLOUR**
- **POTATO FLOUR**
- **GREEN BANANA FLOUR**
- **BREADFRUIT FLOUR**
- **GRAPESEED FLOUR**
- **TIGER-NUT FLOUR**

Vegetable Fern

Diplazium esculentum (Athyriaceae)

ALSO KNOWN AS
Fiddlehead, dhekia, paco,
fougère végétale, pucuk paku,
kuware-shida

NATIVE RANGE
East, Southeast and South Asia

NATURALIZED IN
Africa, Australia, New Zealand,
Papua New Guinea and
North America

GROWING CONDITIONS
Thrives in wet and marshy ground,
forests, rainforests and ditches
and on riverbanks in a range of
humus-rich, reliably moist soils.
In cultivation, plant in frost-free,
warm, typically wet areas, but
also shaded and sheltered spots
in dry areas.

WHERE TO FIND
Readily available in
markets and stores throughout
Asia and Oceania.

HOW TO EAT
The young fronds are rich in
iron, phosphorus, potassium
and protein. Try them in stir-fries,
salads, soups, stews and tempura,
or pickled.

Ferns are one of the oldest groups of plants on Earth. Of the approximately 10,500 species that are alive today, many have been around for 70 million years, and their ancestors go back a staggering 430 million years. They produce neither flowers nor seeds, reproducing instead via spores, and typically favouring moist, shady situations in forests and rock crevices, as well as bogs and swamps. They are extremely diverse, from towering tree ferns 20 metres (66 feet) tall to the tiniest aquatic fern, the size of an adult's fingernail. Humans have been eating ferns for millennia, but not all fern species are edible; in fact, the majority are known or believed to be toxic to varying degrees.

Diplazium esculentum is arguably the most widely consumed and nutritionally analysed of the vegetable ferns. Although it has many colloquial names, a much-used English term is 'fiddlehead', which, although descriptive of the unfurling young fronds (1), is not particularly helpful, being also applied to several unrelated edible species. Demand is such that *D. esculentum* is becoming more widely available, with farmers establishing commercial growing beds shaded from the sun. For those in colder climates wishing to grow fiddleheads, the ostrich fern (*Matteuccia struthiopteris*) is easily cultivated.

The vegetable fern is very tolerant of wet and marshy ground, making it ideal for cultivation on marginal land, such as that prone to flooding. Its ability to thrive in shade makes it a useful choice for the ground-cover layer of agroforestry systems. It also grows rapidly, and as such has the potential to ensure food and nutritional security in many tropical parts of the world.

All edible ferns can be consumed only after proper preparation and cooking. The young fronds (2) must be stripped of their brown hairs and washed in several changes

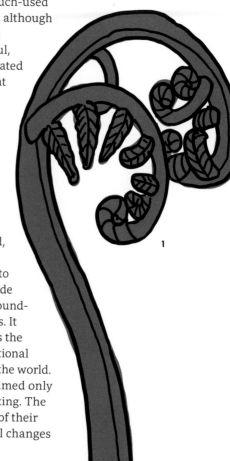

1

2

of cold water before being cooked.
A typical northern Indian recipe using
the vegetable fern consists of chopped
young fronds stir-fried with asafoetida
and cumin seeds and sprinkled generously
with turmeric, red chilli powder and salt,
before being mixed with yogurt curd (*dahi*).
In the Philippines, the young fronds are blanched
briefly and used in a salad with tomatoes, hard-boiled
eggs, thinly sliced onions, vinegar, and a little sugar and
salt. The fronds have a texture that can be crunchy or
slimy, depending on how long they are cooked for, and a
flavour that is reminiscent of asparagus, with a hint of
tangy sweetness.

Ebbing's Silverberry

Elaeagnus × submacrophylla (formerly *E. × ebbingei*)
(Elaeagnaceae)

It's fair to say that of the underused plants bearing edible fruit, none is so well known to so many people than the species and hybrids of *Elaeagnus*. Few even notice them edging the car parks of supermarkets, or as a common hedge and barrier in the landscapes of towns and cities. They are literally beneath our noses, with their sweetly scented, often hidden flowers followed by nutritious fruit. Of the more than fifty species, most come from Asia and southern Europe, with the exception of *Elaeagnus commutata*, a native of North America, from where the common name 'silverberry' originated. About ten species have emerged as popular garden plants that are adaptable to a range of situations and conditions, except waterlogged soil. Once established, they are very tolerant of drought; as a nitrogen fixer, they can grow in poor and polluted soil and, in doing so, support the growth of neighbouring plants. A long – and in some cases ongoing – tradition of use in folk medicine and as food is recorded throughout many cultures of its native range. Despite being cultivated as an exotic ornamental for some 500 years, it is only recently that the silverberry's potential as a commercial food source has been explored.

The evergreen silverberry is an excellent choice for productive shelter belts and windbreaks, and can brave exposed coastal positions. It is also happy in shade, so is ideal for filling out outgrown hedges, or in agroforestry systems as a pruning-tolerant middle layer.

Producing fragrant flowers in the late autumn and delicious fruit in the spring, it is one of the first plants in the garden to bear edible fruit. The flowers have a strong aroma, making them ideal for flavouring desserts, while the fruit is juicy with a somewhat tart flavour reminiscent of wild cherries and redcurrants. It is perfect for a variety of jams and jellies, juices, baked goods, sodas, fruit wines and leathers, and even in savoury stews and chutneys.

ALSO KNOWN AS
The colloquial names of the many species are often applied to this hybrid

NATIVE RANGE
A hybrid of garden origin

GROWING CONDITIONS
Ideal for poor, dry soils of low nutrients in full sun or partial shade. Tolerates exposure to wind and maritime conditions. Fixes nitrogen through its root system, and is hardy to about -25°C (-15°F).

WHERE TO FIND
Most commonly available to buy in Southeast Asia. Silverberries can also be foraged from hedgerows if care is taken to identify them correctly.

HOW TO EAT
The juicy berries are rich in vitamins and minerals and can be eaten raw, made into jams or jellies, juices, sodas and fruit wines, or used in baking.

Mountain Spinach

Elatostema involucratum (Urticaceae)

ALSO KNOWN AS
Mizu, rainforest spinach, dambru, xia ye lou ti cao, himbu

NATIVE RANGE
Asia

GROWING CONDITIONS
Reliably moist, shaded forests and woodlands. Can withstand short periods of drought. Easily propagated and grown in moist shade.

WHERE TO FIND
Sold at markets in Japan, Bhutan and parts of India, in bundles as a leafy vegetable.

HOW TO EAT
Enjoy the crisp, mineral-rich sprouts, stems and leaves in soups, stir-fries, pickles and tempura.

Despite being found as a wild forest plant throughout Australasia, Asia and Africa, the genus *Elatostema* is little studied by science today, but its members may be useful as edibles, medicinally, or both. The naming can be complicated; *E. japonicum* is often used on ingredients labels, and *E. umbellatum* var. *majus* in commerce. The stems are flushed red with glossy green leaflets edged with saw-like toothed margins (1). Clusters of very small white flowers (2) appear in the leaf axils, followed by curious purple bulbils that fall to the ground to produce more plants. Many of the 500-plus recorded species have formed and, in many cases, still form an important part of local diets. There are believed to be as many as 500 more species yet to be recorded, and recent discoveries of cave-dwelling species growing in heavy shade give an example of the genus's diversity. Sadly, many inhabit areas that are at risk of deforestation.

Most species of this non-stinging, herbaceous perennial of the nettle family are to be found in East Asia, South Asia and Southeast Asia, and that is where some of them are considered a culinary delight, being both tasty and nutritious. From a wild habitat of mountainous shaded wetlands and streamsides, it has proved perfectly adaptable to cultivation and supply to both professional and domestic kitchens through distributors and supermarkets. Aomori, a prefecture in the northern part of Japan's main island of Honshu, is the biggest source of cultivated mountain spinach. There it is often grown on otherwise unproductive land, a circumstance that points to its global potential as a productive, heat-resistant edible that tolerates waterlogged and poor, rocky soils as well as deep shade and periods of drought.

The sprouts, stems and leaves are harvestable all year round and can be eaten both cooked and raw. The simple Japanese dish *hoyamizu* consists of peeled and blanched mountain-spinach stems mixed with sliced sea pineapple (sea squirt) in a dashi soup. Having a crisp texture and a fresh, green, faintly floral aroma, mountain spinach can be also used in soups, stir-fries and tempura, and it is delicious pickled.

Enset

Ensete ventricosum (Musaceae)

The banana relative *Ensete ventricosum* is a species of great historic and future food security in Africa. For those outside that continent who wish to bring a little 'exotic' into the garden or home, *E. ventricosum* 'Maurelii' is the go-to plant, with its large, mahogany-red paddle-like leaves. Despite the historical existence of the 'Enset belt', from northeast Lake Victoria southeast to the Usambara Mountains in Tanzania, the cultivation and use of enset have all but disappeared outside Ethiopia. There it is a staple food produced on family-run homesteads, where about fifty plants can support a family of five or six people. Wild plants are considered inedible, so over an estimated 10,000 years of domestication hundreds of cultivated landraces have been selected for different attributes. Every part is used in a process led by the women of the family.

Enset is susceptible to pests and disease, which threaten people's sustenance and livelihoods. In mitigation, and to allow it to be adopted elsewhere in the future, a great deal of work is being carried out locally and internationally. Avoiding monocultures by intercropping with sorghum, maize and coffee, and harnessing genetic diversity in breeding, will help to fulfil the potential of what is known in Ethiopia as the 'tree against hunger'.

Producing a high yield that exceeds that of many starchy staples, even without irrigation, enset is ready for harvest all year long. That makes it a promising crop that could ensure food security for millions of people in sub-Saharan Africa. It is also very nutritious, being high in carbohydrates, minerals and fibre.

Unlike its famous cousin *Musa*, of banana and plantain fame, enset is cultivated for its edible vegetative parts rather than its fruit. The underground corm can be eaten raw or cooked, and the trunk-like pseudo-stems and flower stalks must be cooked and processed before consumption. A popular Ethiopian flatbread known as *kocho* is made of a dough collected by scraping enset's pseudo-stems, and fermented in pits before being steam-baked between enset leaves. It has a sourdough-like taste and releases a strong, cheesy smell while it is being fermented. The enset 'dough' can also be dried, fried, or used for porridge or cakes. The corm meanwhile shares similarities in both texture and flavour with potatoes, and is used similarly in stews and porridges.

ALSO KNOWN AS
Ethiopian banana,
pseudo-banana, false banana

NATIVE RANGE
Eastern sub-Saharan Africa

NATURALIZED IN
Gulf of Guinea islands, Java
and Juan Fernández Islands

GROWING CONDITIONS
A cool tropical climate of high humidity in full sun or partial shade on a range of nutrient-rich soils. Slightly tolerant of wet conditions, and can withstand short periods of light frost and drought. In cold climates it can be managed as an ornamental house or seasonal garden plant.

WHERE TO FIND
Only in Ethiopia.

HOW TO EAT
Try the corm (high in carbohydrates) cooked in stews or porridge.

Culantro

Eryngium foetidum (Apiaceae)

The family Apiaceae, often referred to as the umbellifers, is a diverse group of plants that include vegetables, herbs and spices, among them the ubiquitous carrot, parsnip, celery, angelica, caraway and fennel. Soon to join the ranks of this family's internationally known members is the biennial herb culantro, a native of Mexico and tropical America. It is a cousin of coriander, *Coriandrum sativum*, with which it shares some properties, although the two have a very different habit and leaf. Coriander is known to many as cilantro, and the similarities of these two colloquial names are a source of confusion to gastronomic adventurers and spellcheck alike.

The Latin name of culantro consists of *Eryngium* (a genus perhaps best known for the sea holly) and the unfairly off-putting *foetidum*, which means 'smelling extremely unpleasant or foetid'. However, this epithet is a clue to its main distinction. Culantro is significantly more pungent than coriander, so much so that, unlike its more delicate counterpart, it can be cooked and boiled, rather than being added to food just before serving. It is a tasty seasoning and vegetable, but many ethnomedicinal uses have been recorded throughout the ages to treat conditions as diverse as snake bite and (in contradictory fashion) both constipation and diarrhoea.

Culantro was introduced to China in the nineteenth century and is now in common use there, as it is in Southeast Asia and the Pacific Islands, while such countries as India, Australia and the United States (specifically Hawaii) are also recognizing its commercial and culinary potential. Perfectly adapted to the tropical climate, it can tolerate high heat and shade as well as periods of drought and intense rainfall. These are essential abilities as the world's weather becomes ever more unstable. Hardy and prolific, it is a great commercial crop and as such will soon be available in supermarkets worldwide.

This punchy herb can be eaten both cooked and raw. The quintessential Puerto Rican sauce *sofrito* (sometimes known as *recaíto*) is a blend of onions, garlic, sweet peppers and – the star of the show – a large quantity of fresh culantro leaves. Although it is very similar in flavour to cilantro, culantro's greater intensity allows a broader range of uses as a garnish, in marinades and as cooking-proof seasoning in soups, curries, stews and chutneys.

ALSO KNOWN AS
Racao, Puerto Rican coriander, spiny coriander, chardon étoile fétide, Langer Koriander

NATIVE RANGE
Mexico and tropical America

NATURALIZED IN
Southeast Asia and the Pacific Islands

GROWING CONDITIONS
Forests, disturbed areas, moist and shaded tracks in a variety of soils. In climates of heat and high light levels commercial production is carried out in shade, resulting in larger, greener, more pungent leaves. Although tolerant of light frosts, it is typically grown as an annual in cooler climates.

WHERE TO FIND
Widely in Mexico, South America and India. Seeds can be bought worldwide for cultivation at home.

HOW TO EAT
Use the mineral-rich leaves as a garnish, or in flavourful marinades, soups and chutneys.

Bolivian Fuchsia

Fuchsia boliviana (Onagraceae)

ALSO KNOWN AS
Lady's eardrops

NATIVE RANGE
Northwestern Argentina,
Bolivia and Peru

NATURALIZED IN
Hawaii, California, Mexico,
Jamaica, Guatemala, El Salvador,
Costa Rica, Colombia, Venezuela,
Ecuador, Spain, Madeira, Canary
Islands, St Helena, Réunion, Java
and New Zealand

GROWING CONDITIONS
Grows in cool, moist, mossy
forests at high altitude in a range
of soils. Easily grown in gardens,
where it requires protection from
all but the mildest frosts. Can also
be grown in containers.

WHERE TO FIND
Berries are sometimes available
at regional markets in South
America, or from gardeners
growing ornamental fuchsias
worldwide.

HOW TO EAT
Enjoy the juicy berries or flowers
as they are, or in jams, juices
and preserves.

Native to New Zealand, the Polynesian Society Islands, Mexico and tropical America, plants in the genus *Fuchsia*, of which there are more than 100 species, have been adopted as a cherished ornamental throughout the world. Over little more than 300 years thousands of hybrids have been raised by breeders competing to introduce the latest, greatest flowering sensation. In species, and most hybrids, abundant flowers **(1)** produce abundant fruit **(2)** 5–25 millimetres (³⁄₁₆–1 inch) long, rounded or elongated, in dark red-green, deep red or deep purple. These 'berries' are attractive in themselves, but also – a circumstance that is unknown to all but the keenest gardener – edible, as are the flowers. This revelation will lead any gardener to sample the fruit, but, unless you are lucky, this will be an underwhelming experience since, with rare exceptions, flavour is not a breeding prerequisite. The tastiest fruit have long been treasured by Indigenous peoples throughout the plant's native range, such as the Māori of New Zealand, who enjoy the berries of the tree-like *kōtukutuku, F. excorticata.*

However, it is in South America and the geological microclimates of the Andes that there is the greatest diversity of *Fuchsia*. There, *F. boliviana* has long been revered for its beautiful hanging clusters of vibrant red, long, waxy flowers and tasty red fruit. The Quechua people know it as *coapac-nucchchu*, 'superior salvia', in reference to another flower that was sacred to the Inca. Ancient Andean drinking vessels made from wood, ceramics, silver or gold and known as *qiru* feature a plant that many historians believe to be the Bolivian fuchsia. Although it is hardy in light frost, in cooler temperate climates *F. magellanica* is a more reliable choice for the garden; it is heralded as the hardiest species and is the parent of many hybrids, some of which inherit its flavour.

The Bolivian fuchsia grows vigorously and is a long and prolific bloomer, producing abundant flowers from June well into September. This makes it an important source of nectar for hummingbirds and bees.

The juicy berries are rich in vitamins and minerals. They have a peppery sweetness reminiscent of kiwi and grapes, and can be eaten cooked or raw, while the colourful flowers are a stunning addition to any salad. The regional Chilean fermented alcoholic drink *chicha* is made from them, and they are also used in jams, juices and various preserves.

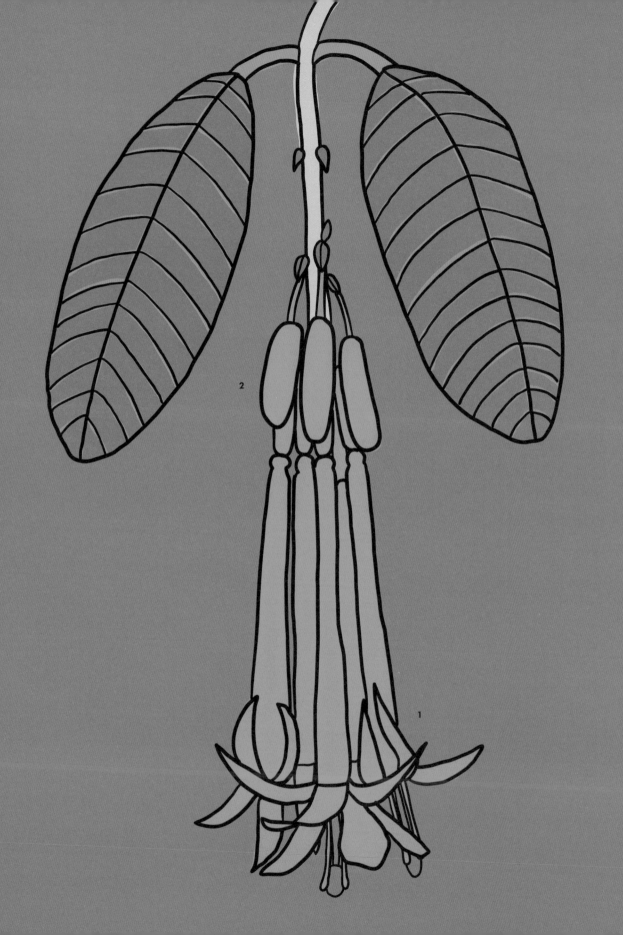

Roselle

Hibiscus sabdariffa (Malvaceae)

3

For many people, hibiscus recalls the tropical paradise of Hawaii, where it's honoured as state flower. However, it is the Chinese hibiscus, *Hibiscus rosa-sinensis*, with its large blooms ranging from white through pink, red, yellow and apricot to orange, that best represents species of ornamental value. Gardeners, particularly those in temperate climates, may be unaware of the long history of medicinal and culinary applications of some hibiscus. Not all are known to be edible, and indeed they can easily be confused with close relatives, so stick to those of common use (among them the Chinese hibiscus).

A species of traditional culinary importance and growing demand is *H. sabdariffa*, commonly known as roselle. This valuable traded plant of antiquity spread from western tropical Africa and Sudan to Egypt, Asia and South America. It is considered a short-lived perennial, and many grow it as an annual that quickly reaches 3.5 metres (11½ feet) in height, its deep-red stems clad in palmate dark green to red leaves, which are consumed when young. White, blush-pink or salmon-pink with a dark red eye, the large, funnel-like flowers (1) appear in long succession from buds encased in protective wine-red sepals (2). These sepals are known collectively as the calyx; they become plump and envelop the developing seed, and are harvested when tender and crisp (3).

Often grown on low-quality land, roselle is a resilient multipurpose crop that can withstand periods of drought. This makes it a useful choice for subsistence farmers worldwide, offering a solution to insecurity of both food and income.

The fleshy calyx, young leaves and stems can be eaten both cooked and raw, while the seeds are roasted and ground into a gluten-free flour. A simple but delicious drink is made by boiling the fresh or dried calyces in water for 10–15 minutes before adding a sweetener

to taste. With a sweet-and-sour flavour reminiscent of cranberries and rhubarb, the calyx can be used in salads, jams, jellies, juices, wine, baked goods and syrup. It also makes a tasty tea, spice or even an addition to granola. The leaves are much like a spicy, rhubarb-like spinach and can be used in the same way as that more widespread vegetable.

Climate Change and Plants

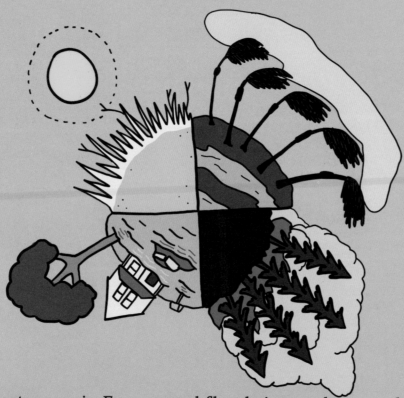

From heatwaves in Europe and floods in southern and eastern Asia to hurricanes in North America, drought in sub-Saharan Africa and wildfires in South America, extreme weather events are becoming much more frequent. But it's not just the extremes. The averages – especially temperatures – are also rising globally and are destined to do so for centuries to come, at a speed and intensity that are inextricably linked to the rate of humans' emissions of greenhouse gases. We may have enjoyed a period of relative climatic stability since the last ice age, but the age of frequent change is now upon us.

This constitutes a monumental challenge for nature as we know it, particularly for plants that are highly adapted to specific conditions. With temperature ranges shifting, often to higher latitudes and/or altitudes, and the availability of water changing, plants must follow suit, a circumstance that has a drastic effect on their distribution. This has consequences for the ecosystems from which they are withdrawing and into which they are moving, often sending both out of balance and leaving them vulnerable to pests and disease, as well as invasive species. This is a cascade of effects that ultimately has a negative impact on plant productivity overall, as well as the fundamental ecosystem functions they provide.

This is a particular challenge for humans' highly complex yet surprisingly fragile food system, which is built predominantly on just a few annual plants, tailored to produce bumper harvests under stable conditions. These plants are now facing climatic instability that they are not equipped to handle. Moving crop zones to higher latitudes and elevations, and adapting plants relatively quickly to changing conditions through targeted breeding methods, are two important pieces of the puzzle, but they can't be employed everywhere or, for that matter, indefinitely. They are also no help in the face of unpredictable extreme weather that affects all crop zones.

Safeguarding our future food supply means turning the focus on crop plants that are very resilient to change, plants that can withstand everything from heat, drought and heavy rainfall to periods of flooding, frost and high wind, all the while producing reliable harvests. Fortunately, there are many that fit the bill, and which, incredibly, already thrive in some of the planet's most challenging environments. When these species are embedded in highly diverse and resilient systems, such as agroforestry, and grown in a rich variety of regionally adapted cultivars, they will enable us to rise to the challenges brought by the age of change.

Sea Buckthorn

Hippophae rhamnoides (Elaeagnaceae)

About 12,000 years ago, as the last great ice age ended, our hunter-gatherer ancestors began a slow transition from nomadic living to permanent settlements sustained by agriculture. They domesticated many wild fruit plants, among them sea buckthorn. It is now relatively unknown, a fact that is all the more surprising because the fruit's nutritional benefits were well documented throughout antiquity. In the fourth century BCE Alexander the Great is said to have noticed that his horses loved the berries, and that, after eating them, they had more strength and shinier coats, recovered more quickly from injury and illness, and seemed to radiate health. To harness that strength and vitality for himself, Alexander incorporated the fruit into his diet, as well as that of his troops. Today science has confirmed ancient wisdom and recognized the plant's nutritional benefits, and it is enjoying a renaissance, being commercially grown in various parts of the world.

A very hardy shrub or small tree, sea buckthorn is adapted to the harshest maritime conditions imaginable, growing on salt-laden sand dunes. Neither gale-force winds nor temperatures of -40°C (-40°F) will keep it from thriving, and even drought and heat of 40°C (104°F) don't put it off its game. Such an ability to survive is a great asset in the face of the extreme weather brought on by climate change. The plant's strong network of roots stabilizes the soil and builds up fertility by fixing nitrogen, making it an excellent choice for land-reclamation projects and living fences.

The fruit and leaves of sea buckthorn can be eaten cooked or raw, while the seeds are pressed to extract their oil. An easy northern European recipe for a warming winter drink involves boiling the fresh berries in water with cinnamon sticks, star anise and honey. The berries can also be used in jams, jellies, juices, cakes and soup. They have a squashy texture and unique slightly sour, tart aroma, with hints of citrus and pineapple. The raw leaves can be eaten in salads, or brewed into an infusion with a flavour reminiscent of a slightly earthy green tea.

ALSO KNOWN AS
Common sea buckthorn, sallowthorn

NATIVE RANGE
Most of Europe, to Siberia and the western Himalaya

NATURALIZED IN
Eastern Europe and parts of North America

GROWING CONDITIONS
Coastlines, riverbanks and terraces, dry riverbeds, forest margins, thickets on mountain slopes and meadows up to 4,200 m (13,800 ft). Prefers a sunny position in moist, free-draining, lightly acidic to alkaline soil, but also grows in wet, semi-shaded areas.

WHERE TO FIND
Available fresh, as juice, as oil or frozen at local markets and speciality eastern European food stores and pharmacies across Europe, Asia, North America and Australia.

HOW TO EAT
Try the berries raw, or in tea, juice or preserves. Tea made from the leaves is high in vitamin C.

Yuki Urui

Hosta (Asparagaceae)

Hostas are hugely popular ornamental garden plants in much of the temperate and subtropical world, famed for the diversity of their foliage and often showy flowers, some of which are sweetly fragrant. Their evolutionary origins have been traced to east-central China, from where they spread into Korea, Russia and – via the land bridges of the last great ice age – Japan. Although these plants were recorded as far back as the Han dynasty of China (206 BCE–220 CE), it is widely considered to be the Japanese who ultimately popularized them. Known as *giboshi zoku*, hostas have been celebrated in the written, visual and culinary arts of Japan since the Nara period (710–94 CE). Working with species and naturally occurring mutations, specialist growers and collectors have obsessively bred and selected thousands of varieties over hundreds of years. Since the nineteenth century, such dedication has inspired Western enthusiasts, particularly those in the United States. Hostas are elegant, typically large-leaved, garden plants for moist shade. This makes them a perfect living mulch for climate-resilient food forests.

It may surprise Western readers that in East Asia hostas are regarded not only as ornamentals but also as having many culinary uses. Indeed, they are a large part of the traditional Japanese *sansai* ('mountain vegetable') cuisine, which refers to plants foraged in the wild. The Japanese traditionally relied on *sansai* to fend off starvation during times of drought or natural disaster, and it was important in the aftermath of the Second World War. Until relatively recently, the genus was considered a wild vegetable, but hostas are increasingly being grown commercially for food.

The shoots, young and mature leaves, leaf stalks and flowers are perfectly edible both cooked and raw. The shoots and young leaves are crisp, with a remarkably sweet flavour similar to early pea pods and young cucumbers. The older leaves and leaf stalks have a firmer, more leathery, fibrous consistency with a slightly bitter taste similar to that of spinach. The shoots and leaf stalks are excellent in stir-fries, lightly steamed or barbecued in the same way as asparagus, while the leaves can be sautéed or used in salads or as wheat-free sandwich wraps. The attractive flowers make a sweet, floral-tasting treat that will decorate any plate.

Sweet Potato Leaves

Ipomoea batatas (Convolvulaceae)

ALSO KNOWN AS
Camote, kuma, Süsskartoffel,
patate douce

NATIVE RANGE
Tropical America

NATURALIZED IN
Much of the tropics

GROWING CONDITIONS
Can grow just about anywhere,
from cool temperate grassland
to warm, wet tropical climates.
Adapted to wide range of soils,
in full sun or partial shade, and
frost-free conditions.

WHERE TO FIND
At markets throughout Africa
and Asia, or from local growers
worldwide.

HOW TO EAT
The leaves are rich in vitamin B
and minerals. Try them in stir-fries,
sautéed, in salads, boiled, as an
infusion or even juiced.

Sweet potato is one of the world's most important food crops.
For many people it is a familiar staple of countless generations,
but for some in cooler temperate climates it is an exotic newcomer.
Its ancestry can be traced back 80,000 years before humans, to
tropical regions of the Americas. Evidence now suggests that the
seeds or swollen roots of *Ipomoea trifida* from this area reached
Polynesia on ocean currents and, through divergent evolution over
centuries, became distinct. Ultimately, the hybridization of the
two led to the sweet potato we enjoy today.

Despite its name, it is not closely related to the potato and is
a root rather than a tuber, although the two have been cultivated
together by many cultures. Remains of both have been discovered
on archaeological sites in the Casma Valley, Peru, and dated to
2000 BCE. Today, besides commercial production, it is increasingly
grown as an edible ornamental with colourful leaves **(1)**, along
with attractive flowers **(2)** that are reminiscent of other members
of the genus, such as the morning glories. Its tolerance of poor soil
and variable weather conditions and altitude (from sea level to
2,500 metres/8,200 feet) – of a value not to be underestimated in a
world plagued by increasing soil degradation and climate change –
has enabled its widespread cultivation. Sensitivity to cold and frost
is a limiting factor, so in cooler climates, hardier cultivars must be
used, and overwintered or protected.

From a culinary perspective, it is not only the root **(3)** that is
of interest. The leaves and young shoots are perfectly edible, and,
because they can be harvested several times a year, their yields

3

are much higher than those of many other green leafy vegetables. They are also much more tolerant of disease, pests, drought and wet conditions. They can be enjoyed both cooked and raw. They have a soft texture, a slightly bitter taste when raw and a sweet, spinach-like taste when cooked. They are excellent in stir-fries, sautéed, used in salads, boiled, as an infusion or juiced. This nutrient-dense food is a staple for traditional peoples in Tanzania, where they are cooked with sardines and served with rice or boiled green bananas.

Take care when cutting the stems: a white sap oozes out that may irritate the skin. It is recommended to wash it off before consumption.

Sweet Bush Mango

Irvingia gabonensis (Irvingiaceae)

For thousands of years *Irvingia gabonensis* under its many colloquial names has been an important tree to the people of western and central Africa, from Senegal to Angola and inland to the Democratic Republic of the Congo. It is in the rainforests of the Congo basin that this majestic tree is at its most impressive, forming a sturdy buttressed trunk some 30 metres (100 feet) tall and a broad crown of glossy evergreen foliage. From March to June attractive, sweetly scented, yellow-centred greenish-white flowers appear in clusters; the petals fall and the ovary swells (1) to form round or oval fruit 5–8 centimetres (2–3 inches) long (2). These are variable in size, shape and colour, some being green or greenish-yellow and others yellow-red. The latter can resemble the fruit of the unrelated mango, *Mangifera indica*, hence some of the much-used common names.

Since about 2010 overseas demand for the nut (3) of the sweet bush mango has grown, largely owing to its much-hyped promotion as a weight-control supplement. Although not entirely without evidence, this detracts from its many culinary uses. The wood is highly sought after and commercially traded under the name 'andok' for use in construction and the making of cabinets, tools and sports equipment. As a result, wild populations are under pressure, and the Gabonese government has implemented a ban on logging until 2034. In the meantime, local and international initiatives promote its sustainable production, ensuring fair trade throughout the supply chain.

Adapted to the wet lowland tropics and growing in a wide range of soils, the sweet bush mango is now among sub-Saharan Africa's most economically important foraged and farmed crops. It is often planted to provide shade and reduce soil erosion, and its fruit is an important non-timber forest product with a bright future – if harvested sustainably.

The fruit and the seed kernel, which is known as dika nut, are edible raw or cooked. A traditional Nigerian recipe, the thick and creamy *ogbono* soup, is made from a mixture of meat and fish, stock (broth), onion, chilli peppers, leafy greens and ground bush mango seeds. The unusual-tasting dika nuts, which have a flavour a little like that of almonds, can also be used to make nut butters and cooking oil, or as a spice. The fleshy, faintly slimy fruit tastes a little like mango and is used in jams, jellies, juices and fruit wines.

ALSO KNOWN AS
Wild mango, African mango, bush mango, dika bread tree, dika nut, Gabon chocolate

NATIVE RANGE
Benin to Uganda and northern Angola

NATURALIZED IN
Neighbouring countries, and India

GROWING CONDITIONS
Tropical evergreen rainforest, semi-deciduous forest, near riverbanks and damp locations in deep, rich soil in light shade to full sun. Requires temperatures ranging from 20 to 38°C (68–100°F).

WHERE TO FIND
Fresh fruit is available only in growing regions, but dika nuts can be found in health-food stores worldwide.

HOW TO EAT
The juicy, vitamin-rich fruit is delicious as it comes, or try it in jellies, jams, juice and fruit wine. The kernels can be eaten raw as a snack, or as nut butter.

Indian Butter Tree

Madhuca longifolia var. *longifolia*
and *Madhuca longifolia* var. *latifolia* (Sapotaceae)

ALSO KNOWN AS
Mahua, mi, illuppai, illipe, honey tree, arbre à beurre

NATIVE RANGE
Disputed; believed to be Nepal, India, Sri Lanka and Bangladesh

GROWING CONDITIONS
Most abundant in hot regions between 28 and 50°C (82–120°F), where it can cope with drought. Dislikes heavy shade, preferring an open situation. Thrives best in sandy soil, but grows across a wide variety.

WHERE TO FIND
Worldwide, from speciality food stores and online.

HOW TO EAT
Try the fragrant, fleshy flower (a good source of antioxidants) fresh or dried as a natural sweetener or gluten-free flour. Use the fruit as a vegetable.

Of the Indian subcontinent's many wonderful trees, the Indian butter tree is among the most revered for its bounty of produce. Between them the two varieties – var. *longifolia* of southern India and parts of Sri Lanka, and var. *latifolia*, which is distributed throughout India – provide livelihoods for countless people. Family rights to harvest the flowers from the wild trees have been established for generations and bring sustainable income to all if managed well; the fruit is left to be eaten freely by people, bats and other wildlife, ensuring seed dispersal. This stout, slow-growing ornamental tree has large oval, pointed leaves that emerge a rich red (1) and mature to dark green before yellowing and falling to conserve water before the dry season. From the tips of the naked branches, huge numbers of rust-coloured buds (2) break to reveal the nocturnal creamy-white flowers, their fleshy petals apparently fused shut (3). The tree was long believed to be pollinated by wind, but recent studies have revealed fruit bats to be a significant pollinator. Each morning, unfertilized flowers fall to the ground and are harvested before wild or domesticated animals can feast on them.

A prominent component of tropical deciduous forests, the Indian butter tree can grow on very poor, even saline soil, which it simultaneously stabilizes and improves by fixing nitrogen. Being highly productive even in times of drought, it is a useful tree for shelter belts and agroforestry treelines.

Rich in nectar, the fragrant flowers can be eaten raw or cooked, as can the fruit, while the seeds provide an edible oil. In eastern India a distilled wine known as *mahuli* is prepared from the fermented flowers. The flowers are also used as a sweetener for many local dishes, and have a unique taste that ranges from sweet caramel to strongly floral. Once dried in the sun they store well and can be ground into flour. The fleshy outer coat of the fruit is used as a vegetable. The seeds are also a source of illipe butter, from which margarine and chocolate are made, and which is often used to adulterate ghee.

Acerola Cherry

Malpighia emarginata (Malpighiaceae)

ALSO KNOWN AS
Guaraní cherry, Barbados cherry, West Indian cherry, crepe myrtle cherry

NATIVE RANGE
Mexico to northern Colombia

NATURALIZED IN
New Caledonia, Peru, Venezuela and many Caribbean islands

GROWING CONDITIONS
Prefers tropical climates in reasonably fertile, dry, sandy, neutral soils in a sunny yet sheltered position, since its shallow roots make it vulnerable to high wind. Tolerates occasional frost, but for high yields, a temperature of around 26°C (80°F) is required, with periodic rainfall. It is grown as an ornamental in climates that stay above freezing in the winter, and in cooler areas as a container or bonsai specimen that can be moved inside.

WHERE TO FIND
Readily available fresh, frozen or as a juice at markets and health-food stores in the Americas, Africa, Asia and Australia.

HOW TO EAT
Try the raw fruit in juices, baked goods, ice cream, jellies, jams, syrups and salsas. It is high in antioxidants and vitamins A, B1 and B2.

Highly ornate, the small but striking pink blossoms of *Malpighia emarginata* are followed by fruit that resembles that of the unrelated common cherry so closely that the two cannot escape comparison, as is reflected in this plant's many common names. There ends the resemblance, however, and the fruit of this medium-sized evergreen shrub of tropical climes is very different from the cherries found in most supermarkets. The most notable distinction between acerola cherry and its namesake, or indeed almost every other fruit, is its vitamin C content, which is up to 100 times that of an orange or lemon. Containing several small seeds, the fully ripe, bright-red fruit is around 80 per cent juice. Those lucky enough to live near a tree can enjoy it freshly picked; commercially, it is frozen or processed within twenty-four hours to retain its nutrients and flavour.

The acerola cherry is a native of Central America and Mexico, where it was a staple of pre-Columbian cultures in the Yucatán Peninsula. These ancient peoples attributed many medicinal properties to it, and science is now beginning to recognize benefits in areas including heart health and the prevention of cancer. Although the fruit has been grown commercially in Brazil since the mid-1940s, it is only recently that demand has grown, driven by the health-food market and the cosmetics industry, which promotes acerola as a trendy ingredient in topical products that are said to encourage youthful skin.

When grown in dry, sandy soil, the plant tolerates high acidity as well as high salinity, and drought is not a problem for it, making it well prepared for the challenges of climate change. Providing a haven for wildlife, particularly butterflies, it can produce up to three crops of fruit a year. It fruits in the third year after planting, offering prospective growers an impressively quick return on investment.

Acerola cherries can be eaten cooked or raw. The texture is juicy and soft, and the flavour reminiscent of a slightly unripe peach, with hints of cherry and apple. A typical Caribbean recipe consists of fresh cherries blended with water, strained to remove the seeds, mixed with lime juice and sugar, and served with ice as a refreshing drink.

Sapodilla

Manilkara zapota (Sapotaceae)

The sapodilla is a very drought-resistant, long-lived evergreen tree 12–18 metres (40–60 feet) tall with strong, hard-wearing, reddish wood so dense that it sinks in water. It is better known today for its delicious egg-shaped fruit 5–8 centimetres (2–3 inches) across, which has brown skin, rather like a kiwi **(1)**. Increasing demand for the fruit has led to plantations in southern Florida and parts of Australia, joining long-established cultivation outside its natural range in tropical America, the West Indies and parts of tropical Asia. However, in its native habitats of southern Mexico, Belize and northeastern Guatemala, it was originally revered for its latex sap **(2)**, one of the earliest 'chewing gums', known as *tzictli* to the Aztec and chicle today.

The Maya and Aztec boiled chicle, moulded it into blocks and cut them into small pieces to chew. In 1866 the former Mexican president Antonio López de Santa Anna is said to have shared a sample with his then secretary, Thomas Adams, in New York. Adams, who was also an inventor and businessman, saw the potential and founded the American Chicle Company, creating the first flavoured chewing gum. Considered the founder of today's chewing-gum industry, Adams made a fortune.

Being a highly adaptable species, sapodilla thrives in a vast range of soils and climates. It will make its home anywhere from a rocky, salt-sprayed shoreline to the middle of a lowland rainforest. Added to this versatility are a heavy yield of fruit twice a year and powerful roots that stabilize soil, making it perfect for tropical or subtropical windbreaks and agroforestry treelines.

The fruit can be eaten cooked or raw, while the gum must be coagulated with heat before it can be chewed. The ripe fruit has a texture similar to that of pears, and intensely sweet, malty flavours reminiscent of brown sugar and molasses. This makes it a great choice for smoothies, jams, jellies, juices, dehydrated fruit snacks and, surprisingly, vinegar. A delicious dessert, chikoo ice cream, is made by blending the peeled and deseeded sapodilla fruit with condensed milk, folding it into whipped cream and freezing it for several hours.

ALSO KNOWN AS
Chicle gum, common naseberry, sapoti, chico, sapotilleir, Breiapfelbaum, chiku, chikoo

NATIVE RANGE
Mexico to Colombia

NATURALIZED IN
Widely in suitable climates

GROWING CONDITIONS
Hot-humid and subhumid tropical forests at low to medium altitude. Grows well in a wide range of climatic conditions, from wet tropics to dry, cool subtropical areas, but needs full sun for the best yield.

WHERE TO FIND
Fruit is available throughout Central America, India, the Philippines, Florida and Thailand; various food products and chicle-based chewing gum can be found in specialized food retailers worldwide.

HOW TO EAT
The fresh fruit (a good source of fibre, carbohydrates and minerals) can be eaten as it comes or used in smoothies, jams, jellies, juices, ice cream and even vinegar.

Indigenous Food Systems

Born of the Age of Discovery, the second half of the eighteenth century brought an explosion of new technology in the United Kingdom, continental Europe, the United States and elsewhere that continues at pace to this day. This Industrial Revolution of science and engineering, funded by colonialism, changed the way we live and eat forever. The resulting growth in population led Western governments to incentivize farmers to use newly developed machinery, pesticides, fungicides and inorganic fertilizers, such as superphosphates. So began industrialized monocrop farming and food security on an unprecedented scale.

Today we reflect on the good and bad of such an approach with the benefit of hindsight and a growing understanding of nature and biological systems. Industrial farming has come at a cost not only (unintentionally or otherwise) to the people of developing countries, who often paid dearly to fund it, but also to the planet. Raising large areas of a single industrial crop has resulted in the loss of biodiversity below and above ground, as well as in the skies, oceans and waterways. The lack of local diversity among crops and surrounding habitats seriously diminishes nature's defence against pests and disease, which can spread quickly, often undeterred by the chemicals that ultimately allowed them the opportunity in the first place.

From early environmentalists to a growing number of scientists and farmers, in the last few decades a shift in thinking has come about, informed by scientific study, especially in such fields as plant and soil biology, archaeo- and ethnobotany. As well as exploring forgotten crops, much has been gained by studying historical and surviving Indigenous food systems, which are often productive and sustainable. Examples include thriving polyculture agroforestry systems in the Amazon; extremely productive floating gardens (*chinampas*) on freshwater lakes in Central America (1); elaborate dry-land pastoralism systems in sub-Saharan Africa; integrated rice/fish systems in Asia (2); and the combined hunting-and-gathering pastoralist systems of the Arctic Circle.

Managing to produce abundant food in sync with nature and preserving – and, in many cases, enhancing – biodiversity while being resilient to many effects of climate change make such approaches the perfect model. This is particularly true when they are combined with the best modern science, technology and infrastructure. Such approaches are already manifesting in what many assume to be 'modern' systems, such as agroforestry, permaculture, urban agriculture, food forests, hydroponics and aquaponics. Together with forgotten or marginalized crops, they are unrivalled systems that will ensure global food security for centuries to come.

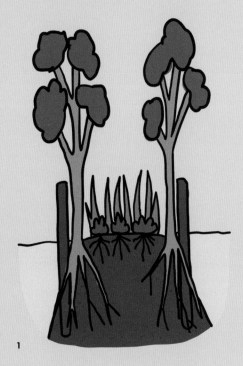

1

2

Spanish Lime

Melicoccus bijugatus (Sapindaceae)

ALSO KNOWN AS
Mamoncillo, genip, quenepa, mamón, limoncillo, huaya, honey berry

NATIVE RANGE
Colombia and Venezuela

NATURALIZED IN
Florida, El Salvador, Costa Rica and several Caribbean islands

GROWING CONDITIONS
Thrives in dry to moist tropical forests in a range of situations and terrains, in a range of well-drained, poor to rich soils including those of high and low acidity. Adapted to drought and tolerant (for short periods) of temperatures close to freezing. Makes a fine tree in cooler climates but seldom fruits in such situations. Plant in partial shade in well-drained soil with additional organic material.

WHERE TO FIND
Local markets and speciality Caribbean and Cuban food stores in the Americas, Africa and parts of tropical Asia.

HOW TO EAT
Try the fruit raw, sprinkled with salt and chilli, soaked in rum and sugar, cooked as a pie filling, or in jams and jellies. The nutritious seeds can be cooked and roasted, or ground into gluten-free flour.

Spanish lime is native to Colombia and Venezuela, where it is a much-loved tree appreciated for its ease of growth, its delicious fruit and the shade it offers from the hot summer sun. There, and indeed throughout much of South and Central America, the Caribbean and beyond, it has become a common tree of streets, yards and smallholdings. Despite its many regional names, it is most often referred to as 'Spanish lime' among English-speakers, especially in the United States, where it is gaining popularity. The fruit, which is smaller than that of the common lime, is similar in shape and colour, but otherwise has more in common with its relative the lychee (*Litchi chinensis*). The outer shell-like skin of the fruit can be cracked open to reveal a pale yellow to salmon-orange gelatinous pulp that is sharp when unripe and deliciously sweet when ripe. The subtle yet pretty heads of white flowers are rich in nectar and loved by both hummingbirds and bees, and the resulting honey is dark and delicious. The fruit hangs in clusters of twelve or more at the tips of the branches, which are removed as a convenient way of harvesting and presenting them for sale. These clusters are a seasonal spectacle, dripping from handsome trees up to 25 metres (80 feet) tall, so much so that they inspire celebration, even among expats. In New York, in a festival that has been held every second Sunday of July since the 1960s, hundreds of Cubans and lovers of Cuban music and dance assemble for the Recordando el Mamoncillo (Remembering the Spanish Lime) festival.

A slow-growing powerhouse, the Spanish lime manages to produce not only intensely tropical-tasting fruit but also a large, nutritious seed. Protected by a leathery skin, both fruit and seed stay fresh for several weeks without the need for refrigeration. This makes the Spanish lime a prime candidate for export and a promising source of revenue for smallholdings across the tropical world.

The fruit can be eaten raw or cooked, while the seeds can be eaten cooked or ground into flour. A delicious Mexican and Caribbean dish, *champola*, is a refreshing frozen treat made from fresh fruit pulp blended with condensed milk, sugar and ice. The fruit pulp has many other uses, and can be boiled in water to makes a tasty juice. Its flavour is a cross between lychee and lime.

The nutritious seeds can be cracked
open and boiled or roasted, like chestnuts.
The Indigenous people of the Orinoco River
consume the cooked, starchy seed as a substitute
for cassava, a fact that hints at its huge potential as
a gluten-free flour or alternative source of starch. The
aroma is similar to the sweet, nutty notes of taro root.

Oysterleaf

Mertensia maritima (Boraginaceae)

From the northern seashores of at least a dozen countries, this humble yet beautiful member of the borage family is migrating to the plates of a growing audience. Its tasty leaves, stem and root stalks have long been foraged by people living in its native range, who enjoy it raw, fermented and cooked. Among them are the indigenous peoples of the Arctic regions of Greenland, Canada and Alaska.

Oysterleaf has great appeal as an ornamental plant, with its low-growing stems of powder-blue, its fleshy, round leaves, and its turquoise-blue flowers that open from pink buds. Its adaptation to extremely harsh coastal conditions allows it to grow just above the high-water mark and makes it tricky, but not impossible, to grow at home. Thriving on salty shingle bars and sandy beaches, anchored by a network of exceedingly strong roots, oysterleaf is a promising candidate for stabilizing eroding shorelines in northern climates. As a plant that is marvellously adapted to the cold, it is becoming extinct in its southernmost localities owing to climate change. Fortunately, oysterleaf seeds – naturally distributed by ocean currents – are easy to germinate, and this has been seized upon by both commercial and domestic producers of microgreens.

The plant's succulent leaves have a juicy texture and a briny, oceanic flavour a little like that of freshly shucked oysters, with a hint of mushroom and seaweed. The leaves and flowers are used in salads and dips, as a garnish or steamed. The flavour is subtle, and can be overwhelmed in very strongly flavoured dishes, so chefs prefer to pair oysterleaf with seafood or serve it simply with crème fraiche. A rich source of nutrients, the plant contains vitamins C and B6, iron, calcium, copper, potassium and antioxidants, and is high in polyunsaturated fats.

ALSO KNOWN AS
Oysterplant, sea bluebell

NATIVE RANGE
Northern Europe, Russia, Greenland and northern North America (from Alaska to British Columbia and Massachusetts)

NATURALIZED IN
Migrating along coastlines away from warming habitats

GROWING CONDITIONS
Grows in free-draining sand, shingle and gravel containing little organic matter. Prefers a cold climate and full sun.

WHERE TO FIND
In supermarkets worldwide.

HOW TO EAT
Try steaming and serving with butter, or eat raw in salads, finely chopped as an ingredient in dips and as a garnish.

Murnong

Microseris walteri (Asteraceae)

ALSO KNOWN AS
Yam daisy, myrnong, garngeg, nyamin

NATIVE RANGE
Australia (except Northern Territory)

GROWING CONDITIONS
Thrives in a wide range of habitats, but most common in the dry, well-drained, sandy soils of open heath forest and grassland. Plant in loamy, moist but free-draining soil in the garden or as a container plant. Adding organic material, compost or natural fertilizer will yield a more harvestable root. Prefers full sun, although it tolerates light shade and temperatures close to freezing.

WHERE TO FIND
Increasingly available across Australia, but still only in small quantities.

HOW TO EAT
Try the roots (rich in carbohydrates) and leaves raw in salads or as a garnish. Roast, bake or fry the roots and mix them with other vegetables, add to soups or puree into a paste for dessert.

The first Australians were semi-nomadic hunter-gatherers, with sophisticated belief systems that encompassed and respected the natural world. Among these Indigenous peoples are the Koori, who originated in a region that equates approximately to what is now Victoria and New South Wales. A large part of their diet is plant-based, of which tuberous roots are a staple. By far the most important of these was once murnong, a member of the daisy family resembling the dandelion. Sweet-tasting when both raw and cooked, it was gathered using digging sticks by women and children, who lifted the plants gently after their spring flowering, removing a portion of the root before replanting the rest. Careful harvesting and controlled burning maintained a never-ending supply of this energy-rich food.

Beginning in 1788, the British colonization of Australia exhibited a shameful, often brutal disregard for the land's Indigenous peoples. One of the many tragic consequences was the near extinction of murnong. In 1841 George Augustus Robinson, the British-appointed 'Protector of Aborigines', noted that the basalt plain was covered with millions of murnong plants, and described women 'spread over the plains as far as I could see them, and each had a load as much as she could carry'. This soon became history as the 'grass rush' of grazing sheep and cattle, not to mention rabbits, decimated the native flora. Today, efforts are underway to reintroduce murnong to wild places, while commercial farms work to supply the emerging bush-food industry.

continues

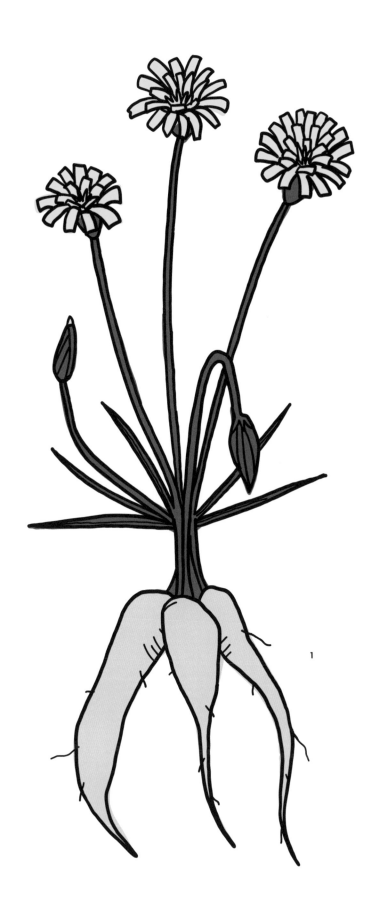

2

3

Able to grow in a wide variety of soils and habitats, murnong is a vigorous perennial herb that could become an important supplier of energy-rich food in many Mediterranean-climate and semi-arid parts of the world. Its highly nutritional underground storage system (1) allows it to thrive in drought- and fire-prone landscapes, and it needs little or no maintenance or input (such as irrigation or fertilizer). There is even increasing evidence that it can grow on reclaimed agricultural sites with permanently raised levels of phosphorus.

Murnong tubers (2) can be eaten cooked or raw, and the leaves (3) – which have a slightly bitter taste – are most commonly eaten raw, in salads or as garnish. The tubers have a crisp, radish-like texture and a flavour akin to that of sweet coconut, with a hint of grassiness. Cooked or roasted, they have the consistency of baked potato, with an accompanying potato flavour that is accented by distinctly nutty, earthy and slightly salty notes. The traditional way to cook the tubers is to roast them in a fire pit or bake them overnight in an earth or mound oven and eat them for breakfast. The long cooking time partially melts them down into a sweet, dark juice.

Moringa

Moringa oleifera (Moringaceae)

Moringa is widely known as the 'miracle tree', and of the fourteen species that are native to tropical and subtropical habitats around the globe, that is an epithet most worthy of *Moringa oleifera*. It originated in the Himalayan foothills of India and Pakistan, where it has been cherished over the centuries for many uses that have, over time, been adopted throughout Asia, Africa, Latin America and beyond. Traditional uses range from medicine, food and cooking oil to natural pesticide, domestic cleaning agent, building material and fodder for livestock. More recent applications include biofuel, and the lifesaving ability of crushed moringa seed to purify dirty water.

M. oleifera is a small, graceful, fast-growing deciduous tree with delicately perfumed cream or white flowers **(1)** followed by fruit, often referred to as pods **(2)**, containing rounded, dark brown seeds 1 centimetre (⅜ inch) in diameter, with three buff papery wings to aid their dispersal by wind or water **(3)**. In cold climates moringa can be grown as a glasshouse container crop or, in domestic situations, kept frost-free over the winter and moved outside in the late spring. To maintain juvenility and ease of harvesting, it can be cut back hard – coppiced – once a year. Its ability to regrow quickly and its all-round durability have earned it the title *nebedies*, 'never-die trees', in parts of Africa.

The ability to grow and be productive in arid regions on a wide range of soils and situations, including old, depleted farmland and areas suffering from desertification, offers huge potential. Furthermore, moringa is little troubled by pests or disease, and can withstand light frosts, making it a versatile addition to any agroforestry system.

Nearly all parts of the tree are edible. The highly nutritious leaves, young pods, immature seeds, roots and flowers can be eaten cooked or raw, and the mature seeds can be ground into flour or processed into an edible oil. Even the tree's gum is used,

continues

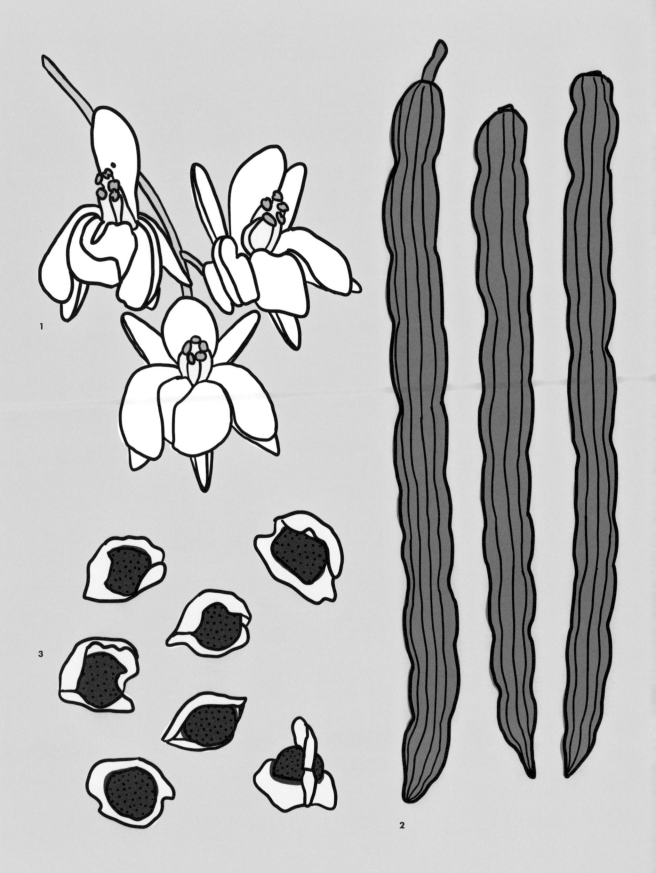

as a food emulsifier. The delicious south Indian stir-fry *murungai keerai thoran* involves sautéing moringa leaves in a spice-infused oil, mixing them with a paste made from fresh coconut, garlic, turmeric and chilli, and serving the resulting dish on rice. The fresh leaves have a slightly bitter, peppery aroma with hints of matcha and rocket (arugula) and are great in soups, stews, curries, fritters and scrambled eggs. A protein-rich powder is made from the leaves, and both this and the gluten-free seed flour can be used in shakes and drinks, as a spice and in baking. Moringa flour has a savoury, mushroom-like flavour and is used in salads, fritters and teas. The root, meanwhile, has a strong, horseradish-like taste and can be used in condiments or sauces. Note that the root is high in alkaloids, so must be eaten in moderation.

Plants in Space

Fertile soil, sunlight and water were the basis of all crops –
until they weren't. It all began with history's first documented
greenhouse, built for the Roman emperor Tiberius in 30 CE to
grow one of his favourite delicacies, snake melon (*Cucumis melo*),
all year round. Consisting of framed slabs of transparent stone,
it was a very early forebear of what would be improved on only
much later – in fifteenth-century Korea – by the addition of a
basic heating system and lightweight windows of oiled paper.
In seventeenth-century Europe, as large sheets of glass became
available, greenhouses began to take a shape that we would
recognize today. Over the following centuries their use spread
rapidly around the world, continually improved upon as new,
lightweight materials became accessible. It was in the 1970s
that the first fully controlled plant-growing environment came
into use, dubbed the phytotron, and that soil was replaced with
various other growing media, such as rock wool.

It was those innovations – with the later addition of hydroponics (whereby plants are grown in a nutrient solution) and energy-efficient LED lighting – that made it possible to grow crops completely apart from the natural world. This gave rise to the concept of indoor vertical farming, an extremely land-efficient modular system that can grow crops vertically under optimal conditions and produce much more food per hectare than traditional farming while using less water and nutrients. Such features make it extremely interesting at a time of climate change, shrinking soil resources, extreme weather, urbanization and a resurgence of interest in space travel.

Although vertical farming is not yet competitive in cost terms with traditional farming, owing to high energy costs and lack of scale, many public and private companies have built successful businesses around it, for now focusing on crops with a high market value, such as microgreens. Cities are exploring its potential as a way of producing fresh vegetables directly in the urban environment, eliminating long supply chains and the associated loss of quality.

Off Earth, the International Space Station has tested a 'Veggie' plant-growth unit, with some success, while research facilities around the world are searching for the most suitable plants for future missions to the moon and Mars. All this is in preparation for a not-too-distant future when Earth is no longer the only plant-growing planet in the solar system.

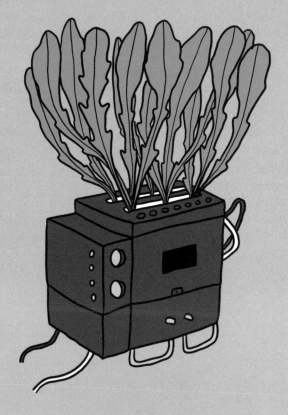

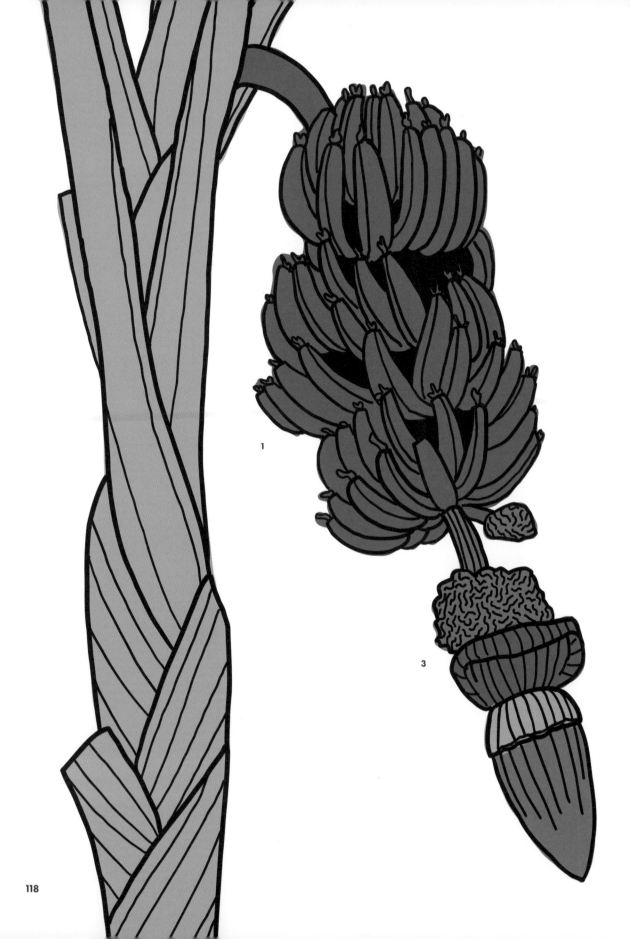

1

3

Red Banana

Musa acuminata (Musaceae)

As one of the world's favourite fruits, the banana is surely a most unlikely candidate for inclusion in this book. The vast majority of bananas that are consumed worldwide are of just one variety – the Cavendish – of which about 55 million tonnes are grown each year. However, there are more than 1,000 varieties of banana; most are underused, but the red banana is becoming increasingly popular.

Botanically a berry, banana fruit ranges from small and round to as long and thick as an average adult's forearm. Some are sweet, some are sour, and they range from very soft to hard. Wild bananas are full of black seeds, making them unpleasant to eat, so, upon finding naturally occurring seedless forms, early farmers set about planting clones of these otherwise sterile plants. About 9,000 years ago the banana became one of humankind's earliest domesticated crops. So began the journey towards the Cavendish variety, and the inevitable consequences of clonal plants and monocrop farming. The world's favourite banana variety is now at risk from a fungal pathogen that is commonly referred to as fusarium wilt, which kills the plants outright. (The Cavendish itself was born of a selective breeding programme to replace the world's first commercial banana, Gros Michel, which was killed by another fungal strain in the 1950s.)

The wild cousins of the banana are more likely to have the genetic diversity and disease-resistance needed for breeders to develop new and improved varieties. Those in the red banana group are typically shorter and rounder than the Cavendish variety, with rosy, red to red-purple skin and soft, pinkish flesh (1). One of the most popular is the commercially produced red dacca, which is found on the island of Mauritius. It has cream- or custard-coloured, semi-soft flesh inside thick red or maroon peel.

Growing very fast in nutrient-rich, slightly acidic soil, red bananas are a great starter plant for tropical agroforestry systems. Quickly producing a cash crop, as well as copious amounts of fast-to-decompose biomass, they are a valuable resource for both the farmer and the soil.

Banana shoots (2), the banana heart (the tender core of the trunk) and banana flowers (3) must be soaked in acidulated water (water with added lemon juice, vinegar or another acid) before consumption. Even the peel is edible after brief cooking.

Ripe red bananas (4) have a sweet, slightly earthy, tropical aroma with hints of raspberry, mango and vanilla, making them notably different from yellow bananas. It is recommended either

continues

ALSO KNOWN AS
Claret banana, Jamaican red

NATIVE RANGE
Much of the Indian subcontinent, Sri Lanka and Southeast Asia

NATURALIZED IN
Florida, Costa Rica, Trinidad and Tobago, Ecuador, Juan Fernández Islands, Spain, Canary Islands, Turkey, Senegal, Tanzania and several islands in the western Pacific

GROWING CONDITIONS
Thrives in moist tropical regions with an average temperature of 27°C (80°F), in nutrient-rich, slightly acid soil that is reliably moist but free-draining. Prefers full sun or partial shade. For successful cropping, bananas must be grown in equatorial regions, but with considered positioning and care, the fruit can be harvested in cooler climates.

WHERE TO FIND
All edible parts are increasingly available from specialized grocers throughout Australasia, Southeast Asia, Africa and the Americas.

HOW TO EAT
Try using the ripe fruit (rich in carbohydrates) in desserts. The peel can be used as a pulled-pork alternative, the stem in stir-fries and juices, the flowers in stews and salads, the shoots as an asparagus equivalent, and the leaves as flavour-giving wraps or eco-friendly plates.

to cook the unripe fruit – since the raw flesh is grainy, dry and chalky – or to grind them into a nutritious gluten-free flour. A favoured Mauritian dish consists of a mixture of coarsely mashed ripe red bananas, vanilla seeds, brown sugar and salt, which is thickened over a medium-low heat before being used as a delightfully tropical-tasting tart filling. Unripe red bananas, on the other hand, are peeled, grated, deep-fried and seasoned with salt and/or spices to create deliciously savoury chips or crisps.

Banana hearts, shoots and flowers have a distinctive flavour that is reminiscent of artichoke, heart of palm and bamboo shoots, with an additional subtle floral taste. A favourite ingredient of traditional south Indian home cooking, banana hearts are used in curries, stir-fries, soups, chutneys and even juices. Banana shoots, meanwhile, are treated in the same way as asparagus. In Indonesia, for example, they are roasted in hot ashes. Banana flowers have a texture that is sometimes compared to fish, and are used to make fritters in Sri Lanka, stews in the Philippines and the tasty salad *yam hua plee* in Thailand.

The leaves, while not directly edible, are often used to wrap various foods for boiling, roasting or steaming, and they impart a subtly sweet, earthy aroma to any dish that is treated in this way. Finally, organic banana peel is a fantastic vegan alternative to meat-based dishes. Scraped clean, shredded with a fork, sautéed briefly and mixed with barbecue sauce, it makes a great 'pulled pork'.

Yangmei

Myrica rubra (Myricaceae)

From Alaska to the Azores, Belgium to Burundi, Venezuela to Vietnam, an alphabet of regions and countries can be quoted when referring to the cosmopolitan genus that is *Myrica*. The forty-nine recorded species, which are variously low-growing shrubs to small trees, are widespread in subtropical and temperate climates. The scientific name is derived from the Greek for perfume or scent, in recognition of the plant's resinous aromatic properties (of which 116 compounds have so far been isolated).

Despite such vast distribution, little variability has been found in the species' active compounds, so it's no wonder humankind has used its many properties in such similar ways. For example, the Indigenous peoples of North America have *M. cerifera*, while those of the Scottish highlands and islands have *M. gale*, but both have used their particular species to make medicine, candles and pesticides. The different species also share culinary applications, as a seasoning and a beer additive to generate foam and flavour. Many are grown for their ornamental use as well as their economic value as a source of paper and rope from the bark, as wood for fuel, for biomass and for their fruit. The ability to produce copious quantities of nutritious berries while also building up soil fertility through an association with nitrogen-fixing root-nodule bacteria and stabilizing the soil makes yangmei a promising crop for infertile hill slopes.

Of those grown for fruit, *M. rubra*, yangmei, and its cultivars are of great commercial importance, especially in their native China. The spherical summer fruit of the female plants is typically 1.5–2.5 centimetres (½–1 inch) in diameter and made up of many fleshy segments, typically crimson but also white or purple, with similar- or lighter-coloured flesh. The fruit, which surrounds a cherry-like seed, will ripen only on the tree, making harvesting and transport difficult; this has led to a concentration on local processing into products that are suitable for export.

The fruit can be eaten raw or cooked. The berries have a slightly pulpy texture and a sweet, tart flavour somewhere between that of strawberry, cranberry and pomegranate, making them a perfect ingredient in jams and jellies, syrups, juices and fruit wines. A refreshing Chinese summer liqueur known as yangmei wine is made by soaking the ripe berries for several months in a clear rice- or sorghum-based spirit; it is drunk with ice on hot days.

ALSO KNOWN AS
Japanese bayberry, red bayberry, Chinese bayberry, yumberry, waxberry, Chinese strawberry

NATIVE RANGE
China, Korea and Philippines

NATURALIZED IN
Mariana and Bonin islands

GROWING CONDITIONS
In forests on mountain slopes and valleys in semi-shade or full sun. Hardy to at least -6°C (20°F).

WHERE TO FIND
Farmers' markets throughout the growing regions.

HOW TO EAT
Enjoy the tasty berries (rich in vitamin C and flavonoids) fresh or made into jams, jellies, syrups, juice or fruit wine.

Nutmeg

Myristica fragrans (Myristicaceae)

ALSO KNOWN AS
Mace

NATIVE RANGE
Maluku

NATURALIZED IN
Gulf of Guinea islands, Réunion, Mauritius, Comoros, Assam (India), Bangladesh, Laos, southern and central China, Thailand, Vietnam, Philippines and Java

GROWING CONDITIONS
Grows wild on rich volcanic soil in hot, humid lowland tropical rainforests. Cultivate in rich, moist, neutral to lightly acid soil in full sun or dappled shade, sheltered from wind in a frost-free climate; mature specimens can tolerate light frosts. Trees fruit at between five and ten years of age, depending on conditions.

WHERE TO FIND
Available fresh or candied at markets throughout its growing regions.

HOW TO EAT
Use the fruit (rich in antioxidants) in juices, jams, jellies or ice cream, or as a baking ingredient.

Throughout history humankind has sought out edible plants and their fruit, and respected, protected or cultivated them to ensure future food security. Of course, where there is value, there is opportunity, and what may begin as a sustainable local endeavour is all too often corrupted by greed. An example is provided by *Myristica fragrans*, of the Banda Islands in the Indonesian province of Maluku. This handsome evergreen tree has pear-shaped fruit (1) that split open when ripe (2) to reveal a striking purple-brown shiny seed covered in an irregular net-like aril of vivid red (3). The seed or nut (4) is typically ground into the spice nutmeg, while the aril (5) is dried and sold as mace.

These two, and the clove of the tree *Syzygium aromaticum*, became popular spices throughout the world via Arab traders, who guarded their origin closely. This monopoly was broken when the Portuguese explorer Vasco da Gama rounded the Cape of Good Hope in 1497 and discovered what became known as the Spice Islands. Tragically, many of the Indigenous peoples of these islands, including those of Banda, were massacred during the Dutch–Portuguese War (also known as the Spice War) in the seventeenth century. Later, the British entered the fray and took over the island of Rhun from the Dutch. In 1674, after several skirmishes, the British agreed to a trade whereby Rhun was returned to the Dutch in exchange for New Netherland, now known as the state of New York in the United States.

Today nutmeg and mace are widely cultivated, mainly in Asia,

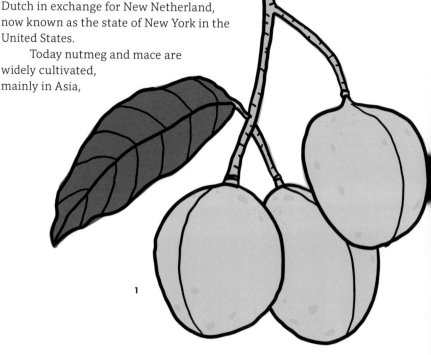

1

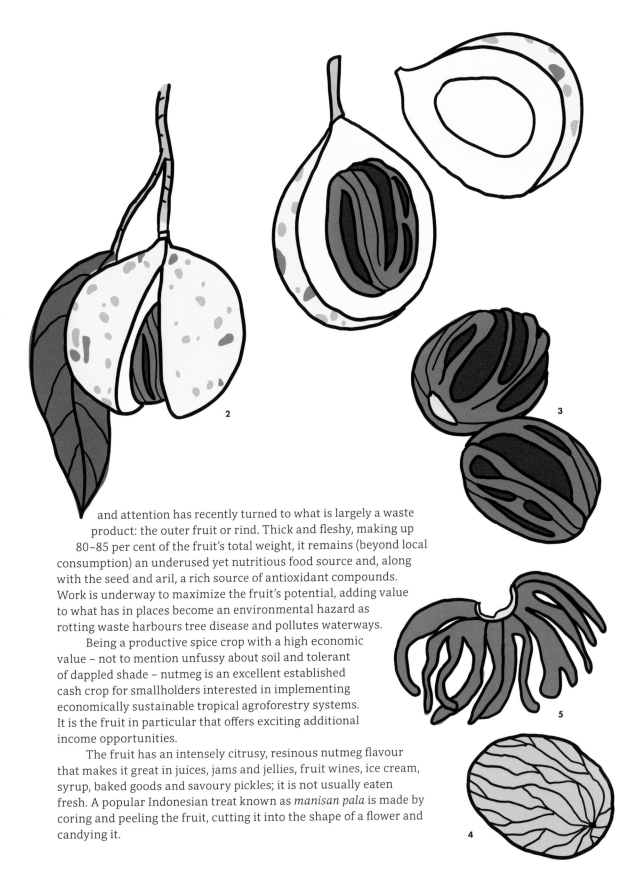

and attention has recently turned to what is largely a waste product: the outer fruit or rind. Thick and fleshy, making up 80–85 per cent of the fruit's total weight, it remains (beyond local consumption) an underused yet nutritious food source and, along with the seed and aril, a rich source of antioxidant compounds. Work is underway to maximize the fruit's potential, adding value to what has in places become an environmental hazard as rotting waste harbours tree disease and pollutes waterways.

Being a productive spice crop with a high economic value – not to mention unfussy about soil and tolerant of dappled shade – nutmeg is an excellent established cash crop for smallholders interested in implementing economically sustainable tropical agroforestry systems. It is the fruit in particular that offers exciting additional income opportunities.

The fruit has an intensely citrusy, resinous nutmeg flavour that makes it great in juices, jams and jellies, fruit wines, ice cream, syrup, baked goods and savoury pickles; it is not usually eaten fresh. A popular Indonesian treat known as *manisan pala* is made by coring and peeling the fruit, cutting it into the shape of a flower and candying it.

Prickly Pear

Opuntia ficus-indica (Cactaceae)

The offer in Mexico of a refreshing 'tuna smoothie' might be more than a little off-putting, until you learn that *tuna* is the local name for the fruit of the prickly pear. It joins the dragon fruit (*Selenicereus undatus*) as one of the most commonly commercially grown and consumed edible cacti. Typically the size of an average lemon, but shaped like a pear, the prickly pear comes in green, white and shades of yellow, red and purple. It has a sweet, slightly acidic flavour that has been enjoyed for millennia by humans from the earliest foragers to today's Latin Americans, for whom it is a staple fruit.

Historically, prickly pears were a convenient food for the prevention of scurvy aboard ship, and as a result they spread quickly far and wide, aided by their ability to take root easily after being discarded or planted in accommodating conditions. Many countries now consider this an invasive species, so care must be taken if it is introduced. Not surprisingly, the earliest growers began the process of selecting spineless plants, and farmers benefit from this today. However, many prickly pear cacti retain varying amounts of clustered, barbed bristles, which are painful irritants to harvesters and chefs alike, although cactus paddles are typically sold prepared, with their bristles removed.

Seen as an important future food for the warming climate, prickly pear is now grown commercially. It provides a low-input, high-yield, year-round income and a food source to enhance the diets of farmers and their livestock. It can withstand temperatures of up to 65°C (150°F) and is extremely resistant to drought. Growing in the most challenging dry soils, such as sand dunes, prickly pears can be used simultaneously as a windbreak and as a living fence that provides a barrier against moving sand. The thick root mats not only anchor the soil and prevent it from eroding, but also die off and regrow rapidly, enriching the topsoil with organic matter. These properties make planting groves of prickly pears one of the most promising ways to rehabilitate desertified ecosystems.

Prickly pear fruit, young paddles, flowers and buds can be eaten cooked or raw, while the seeds and mature paddles can be turned into flour. A typical Mexican recipe consists of de-thorned young paddles – *nopales* – which are quickly grilled and smoked over an open fire, cut into strips, fried in a pan with onions, jalapeño chillies, tomatoes, salt and pepper, and used as a deliciously smoky taco filling. Other uses include eating the paddles raw in salads, frying them, breading them, adding them

ALSO KNOWN AS
Cactus pear, Indian fig, Christian fig, spineless prickly pear, barbary fig

NATIVE RANGE
Mexico

NATURALIZED IN
Widely in suitable climates

GROWING CONDITIONS
Thrives in semi-arid and arid regions with mild, largely dry winters of erratic rainfall, followed by long, hot summers. Grows in typically poor soil, including that subject to erosion, but is unable to withstand salinity, waterlogged soil or frost. Plant in sandy or very well-drained soil. Grows best in full sun.

WHERE TO FIND
All edible parts are increasingly available at local markets worldwide.

HOW TO EAT
Try the young paddles and buds raw, in salads, fried with eggs, breaded, boiled or pickled. The fruit (rich in vitamin C and fibre) can be eaten raw, juiced, or used in ice cream or jam (jelly). The seeds and mature paddles can be used to make gluten-free flour and the flower petals as an edible decoration.

continues

to stews and even pickling them. The texture is fresh and crunchy, with a little sliminess akin to that of okra, while flavours range from green beans, spinach and asparagus to green bell pepper and citrus. The gluten-free flour made from mature paddles can be used in baking. The flowers make a tasty treat that looks fantastic on any plate, while the succulent, crunchy buds can be used in salads and stir-fries, or grilled (broiled), steamed or boiled. The taste and texture are similar to those of the young paddles, but the buds are slightly milder in flavour.

The versatile fruit can be peeled and eaten fresh or juiced, or used in numerous sweet treats, alcoholic drinks and savoury dishes. It has a soft, spongy texture and a unique flavour reminiscent of watermelon with hints of strawberry, banana, citrus and even bubblegum.

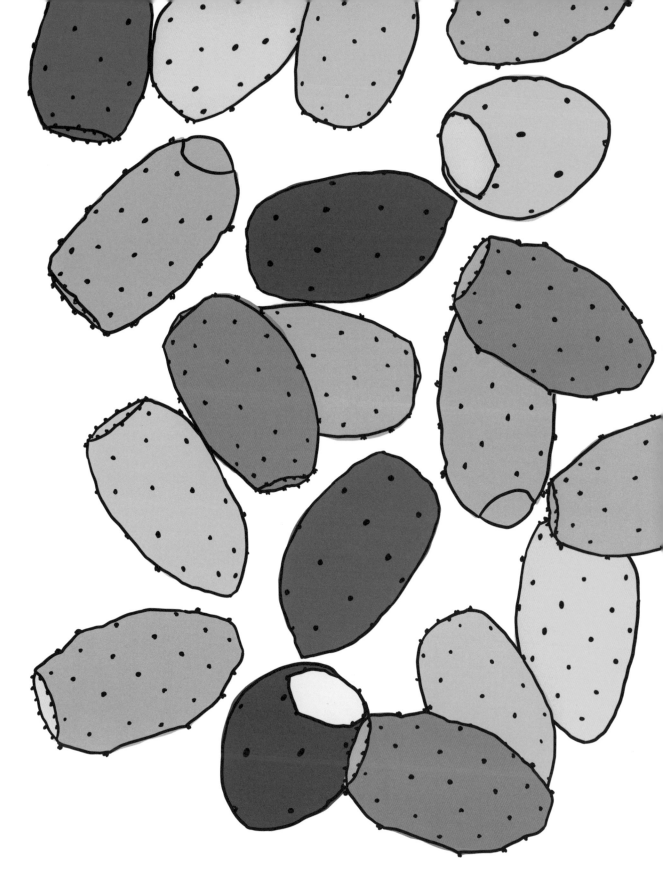

African Rice

Oryza glaberrima (Poaceae)

ALSO KNOWN AS
Red rice

NATIVE RANGE
West Africa

NATURALIZED IN
China and South America

GROWING CONDITIONS
Full sun, between 25 and
35°C (77–95°F) for best
cropping. Prefers fertile soil,
but tolerates a range of soils
with sufficient moisture. Self-
fertile, and typically reaches
harvest 120 days after harvest,
depending on conditions.

WHERE TO FIND
Increasingly available at
markets and shops throughout
West Africa.

HOW TO EAT
Use the kernels as you would any
other type of rice.

Rice has for millennia been one of the world's most important food staples, and it will surely continue to be. From paddy field to plate, it is inextricably linked with Asia, where evidence from such archaeological sites as Huxi, in the lower Yangtze River basin, China, has dated plant remains and evidence of cultivation ditches to about 7000 BCE.

From a wild ancestor of southern and southeastern Asia came the cultivated species *Oryza sativa* that today features in the daily diet of more than half the planet's population. But there is a second, little-known domesticated rice species that belongs to Africa. Independent of its Asian relative, *O. glaberrima* arose as a cultigen of wild *O. barthii* between two and three thousand years ago (1). As the Saharan climate became progressively drier and cooler, beginning about 70,000 years ago, wild rice was relegated to surviving wetlands, forcing farmers to develop sophisticated cultivation techniques, such as flood irrigation and genetic selection, to maintain production. Widely known as African rice (2), this species once helped to feed much of the continent, right up to the emergence of European colonialism and subjugation. It initially spread overseas, particularly to the Americas, as a pioneer species or, very likely, to feed victims of the insidious slave trade. However, commerce and colonial appropriation ultimately led to the higher-yielding Asian species dominating African cultivation.

continues

2   3   4

Although increasingly rare, African rice persists in dispersed locations, partly owing to its value in the sacred rituals of the Jola people of southern Senegal, and to smallholders who prefer its flavour.

For many, African rice falls short of the refinements required for mass production, but it does have several distinct advantages over its Asian counterpart. It is more resistant to some shared pests and diseases, and more tolerant of flooding, infertile soil, extreme weather and human neglect, and its wider leaves shade out competing weeds. Not only can these traits be developed within the many varieties, but also, through hybridization with Asian rice, they can future-proof this important grain.

The rice kernel **(3)(4)** is cooked, puffed or ground into flour. When steamed, it is used as an accompaniment for such dishes as the favourite West African *maafe*, which consists of various meats cooked slowly together with peanut butter, sweet peppers, spices and a mix of root vegetables. Having a red colour and a distinctively nutty flavour, African rice is also used in the production of sweet meats, porridge, puddings, syrups, cakes and other baked goods, and rice flakes for breakfast cereals.

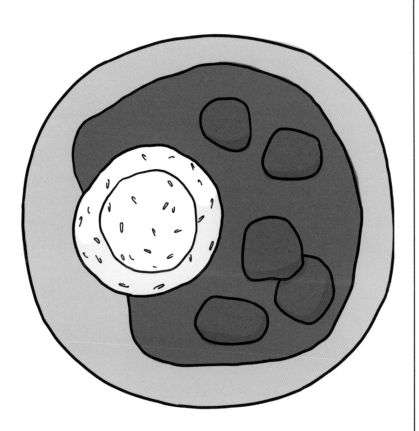

Safou

Pachylobus edulis (Burseraceae)

ALSO KNOWN AS
Native pear, bush butter tree, African plum, shoue, tso, safoutier, uva del país

NATIVE RANGE
West and Central Africa

NATURALIZED IN
Malaysia and Honduras

GROWING CONDITIONS
Humid tropical non-flooded forests in the shade of other trees. Adapted to and tolerant of a range of soils, rainfall and temperature, but must be kept frost-free.

WHERE TO FIND
At markets throughout West and Central Africa, and increasingly at Cameroonian, Nigerian and Gabonese food stores worldwide.

HOW TO EAT
The fruit is rich in polyunsaturated fat, proteins and minerals. Try it roasted, steamed, fried, stuffed or baked.

Safou is a common fruit tree of the West African Gulf of Guinea region, where it is a symbol of fruitfulness and peace for the Yoruba people, sustaining both body and spirit. It is revered for producing tasty fruit during the 'hungry season' between harvests. The branched heads of numerous small, rusty-coloured, fragrant flowers appear in the dry season. Between eight and twelve weeks later, depending on the cultivar and conditions, the highly ornate fruit appear, pale pink or lilac-purple, shiny, rounded oblongs about 9 centimetres (3½ inches) long. The cultivated trees – which are shorter, at typically 10 metres (33 feet) tall, than the wild trees – are an arresting sight when laden with fruit transitioning through ripening colours. Safou is traditionally cultivated in home gardens and small family plantations, and any surplus sold for a good price at local markets. Every part of the tree is used, whether as food, fodder, medicine or building material.

Safou is considered a perfect agroforestry subject to grow alongside cacao and coffee, and today, with improved transport infrastructure, the fruit is being grown for export throughout Africa and beyond, especially in Europe, where expat communities drive demand. Being the source of an edible oil that is favoured by the food, pharmaceutical and cosmetics industries, as well as producing large amounts of fruit that are high in calories and nutrients, it is an ideal multipurpose cash and livelihood crop for farmers.

The fruit can be eaten cooked or raw, although the former is generally preferred. A favourite Cameroonian way of preparing it is simply to cook the colourful fruit in boiling water before sprinkling it with salt and eating it with cassava, fufu or maize. It can also be roasted, steamed, fried, stuffed and baked, or preserved by drying the boiled pulp in the sun. Safou has a slightly sour, tangy flavour reminiscent of olives; that mellows when it is cooked, and the texture is buttery, akin to that of an avocado.

Jicama

Pachyrhizus erosus (Fabaceae)

Jicama, a vine with attractive scented flowers (1), is well known throughout Latin America and has been cultivated since the pre-Columbian civilizations of the Aztec and Maya, while ancient trade routes brought it to the Caribbean and much of Asia. A high-yielding crop of the subtropics, even in the poorest soils, it is naturally nitrogen-fixing. While this tasty, nutritious root vegetable (2) is safe to eat, the growth above ground is toxic to humans; it contains the natural insecticide rotenone, which stymies pests and disease and can be processed for use on other crops. Scientists and botanists recognize the potential of jicama as a sustainable, low-input food for both local consumption and export. And, through selective hybridization, the five *Pachyrhizus* species contain genetic cues that could lead to high yields in a greater range of growing conditions.

Thriving in both tropical and arid climates, jicama has huge potential to improve food security globally. Its exceptional resistance to drought and its nitrogen-fixing properties also promise to mitigate against climate change-induced extreme weather events and soil degradation.

The sizeable tubers can be eaten cooked or raw; any other part of the plant is toxic. In Mexico, two major types are cultivated: *jícama de leche* and *jícama de aqua*. The former has slightly darker skin and white, milky juice (*leche* is Spanish for milk), while the latter has lighter skin and a clear juice (from *aqua*, 'water'). Both are usually eaten raw; expect a crunchy, apple-like consistency with a slightly sweet flavour. In a typical Mayan recipe, peeled jicama is cut into small sticks, mixed with slices of orange, mandarin and grapefruit, and seasoned with chopped habanero chilli, coriander (cilantro), salt and lime juice. It is also a choice ingredient in a host of salads, pairing well with everything from mango, avocado and apple to watermelon, tomato and pineapple. Spiralized raw, jicama is a great gluten-free noodle replacement. When cooked, its flavour diminishes somewhat, leaving a starchy texture and a slight nuttiness.

ALSO KNOWN AS
Chop suey bean, sweet turnip, Mexican yambean, Mexican potato, turnip bean

NATIVE RANGE
Central America, from northwestern Costa Rica to southern Mexico

NATURALIZED IN
Widely in suitable climates

GROWING CONDITIONS
Thrives on deciduous forest edges and in shrubby vegetation on varying soil types from deep clay to sandy loam. Favours the semi-arid tropics with an annual dry season and temperatures of 20–30°C (68–86°F). Plant in well-drained, sandy soil in areas with consistently warm temperatures. To maximize the growth of tubers, remove the flowers.

WHERE TO FIND
Available in the produce section of supermarkets and Mexican grocery stores in the Americas, Australasia, Africa, Southeast Asia and China.

HOW TO EAT
Rich in fibre, vitamin C and minerals, try it raw, sprinkled with chilli powder and lime as an appetizer; in a mixed citrus fruit, mango, pineapple or tomato salad; or spiralized as a gluten-free 'noodle'. Cooked, jicama makes fantastic chips (fries).

Plant-based Foods

THE WORLD'S TOTAL AGRICULTURAL LAND

80% used for
livestock

CALORIES
Livestock
provides less
than 20%
of the world's
calories

PROTEIN
Livestock
provides barely
40% of the
world's protein

KEY

Livestock   Remaining

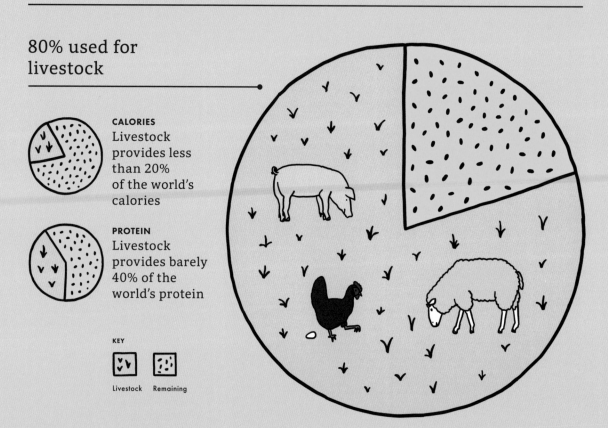

Making the case for plant-based foods can be approached from
a multitude of angles. One of the most convincing, however, has
to be one number: 80 per cent. This is how much of the world's
total agricultural land is used for livestock, either directly for
grazing, or to produce animal feed. Yet livestock provides less
than 20 per cent of the world's calories and barely 40 per cent
of its protein. These numbers simply don't add up.

It is already the case today, then, that plant-based foods feed the world, and that they do so in a way that is significantly better for the environment, the climate and ultimately human health than mass-produced meat. But there is the potential for much more. Switching ever larger parts of our diet to plants will allow us comfortably to meet the demands of a growing population. If this approach were embraced by the world's fifty-four high-income nations, an area of land larger than Europe could be taken out of agricultural production and returned to its natural vegetation. Yearly emissions of agricultural greenhouse gases would drop by a whopping 60 per cent, while the regrowth of highly diverse ecosystems would not only aid biodiversity but also sequester substantial amounts of carbon.

There is no reason for such diversity to exist only off the field. With up to 300,000 edible plants at our disposal, we can already create highly productive agricultural systems that rival nature's abundance in every way. If we add to that advances in science and food technology that allow us to create alternative sources of protein, such as plant-based meat and dairy products, our daily choice of food will be beyond exciting. Bursting with new flavours, textures and aromas, plant-based foods can convince even diehard meat fans to eat more plant-based foods, saving the environment, the climate and our very health as they do so.

Here are a few ways you can add delicious plant-based foods to your diet:

1. Check out the vegetarian and vegan dishes first when looking at a menu. You will be surprised at how tasty they have become.

2. Put vegetables, fruit, cereals and legumes front and centre when deciding what to cook.

3. Get inspired by the sheer diversity of vegetables, fruit, cereals and legumes when shopping. If there is one that you don't recognize, why not quickly search online for its name plus the word 'recipes'?

4. If cooking isn't your thing, there is a bounty of delicious ready-made meals that are vegetarian or vegan. Give them a chance.

5. Become a salad master! There is nothing plant-based that can't be made into a mouth-watering salad.

6. Always have a bowl of fruit on the table and eat it for dessert.

7. Find out more about cooking and eating legumes.

8. Grow your own edible plants.

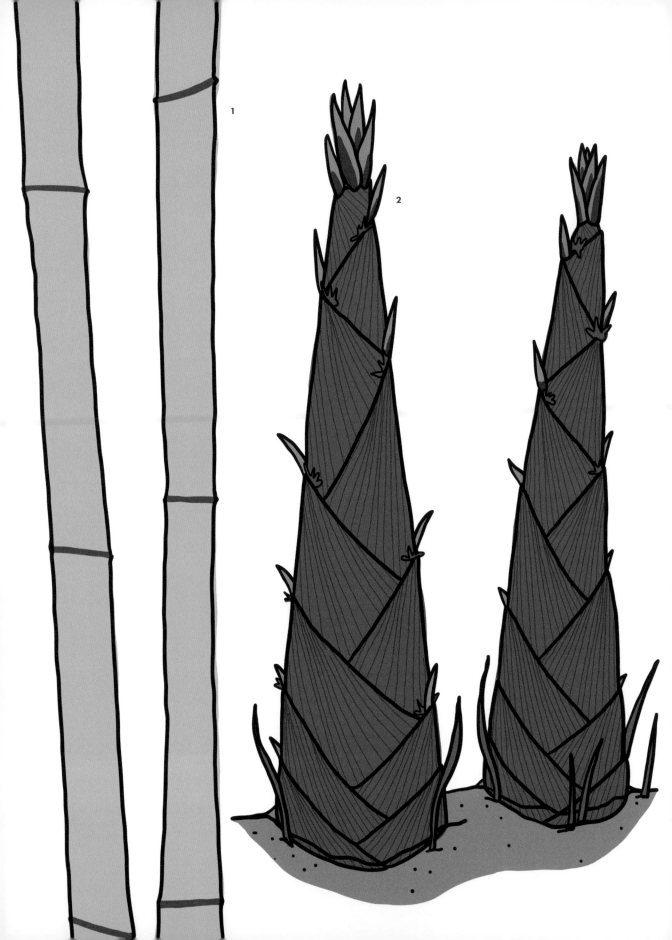

Henon Bamboo

Phyllostachys nigra var. *henonis* (Poaceae)

For most people, bamboo is synonymous with Asia. Indeed, many of the 115 known genera and around 1,700 species are found there and have featured for millennia in local cuisine, literature, art and architecture. But more generally, bamboo is native to tropical, subtropical and mild temperate regions of the world, including the United States, whose only bamboo genus, *Arundinaria*, is also put to great use by Indigenous peoples. From less than knee-high to those forming forests of tree-like proportions, bamboos – actually members of the grass family – have supported and continue to support a huge diversity of life, including the great pandas of China and the mountain gorillas of Central Africa.

About 100 species of bamboo are known to be edible, of which only a handful are commercially grown, and even fewer make it to the export market. Most notable among those is moso bamboo, *Phyllostachys edulis*. However, there is now a great deal of interest in cultivating hardier species, since, although moso is frost-hardy, it doesn't produce a reliable harvest in colder climates. Henon bamboo, *P. nigra* var. *henonis*, is a viable alternative. Its dusky green-grey canes, more correctly known as culms (1), can exceed 15 metres (50 feet) in height, and it is hardy to at least -20°C (-4°F) in sheltered positions. The young shoots (2) taste best; they are harvested shortly after they emerge by excavating and cutting them off at up to 30 centimetres (12 inches) long.

Although bamboo has a bad reputation for invasively overgrowing vast swathes of land, it is actually a powerful tool for mitigating climate change. Being one of the world's fastest-growing grasses, it can quickly absorb and incorporate copious amounts of carbon dioxide into its culms, which, once used as a versatile building material, lock away that carbon for centuries. Managed bamboo forests planted on marginal land thus sequester more carbon, opening up possibilities for farmers to earn revenue from carbon markets as well as from the sale of bamboo material and its edible shoots.

The shoots are high in fibre and vitamins and have a tender, crisp yet slightly fibrous texture and earthy, sweet, nutty flavours reminiscent of baby corn. They are best eaten grilled (broiled), roasted, steamed or pickled. In a popular Chinese recipe, bamboo shoots are peeled and sliced, then stir-fried with ginger in sesame oil before being braised in light and dark soy sauce, rice wine, sugar and stock (broth).

ALSO KNOWN AS
Giant grey bamboo, Schwarzrohbambus

NATIVE RANGE
South-central and southeastern China

NATURALIZED IN
Hawaii, Japan, Vietnam, Philippines, Korea and northern New Zealand

GROWING CONDITIONS
In open forests, on slopes and in valleys on a range of rich, moist but not waterlogged, acid to slightly alkaline soils. Full sun or partial shade.

WHERE TO FIND
Available worldwide, either fresh (through speciality food retailers), or dried or pickled from most supermarkets.

HOW TO EAT
Enjoy the fresh, rehydrated or pickled shoots (rich in fibre and vitamins) in stir-fries, grilled (broiled), steamed or roasted.

Tomatillo

Physalis philadelphica (Solanaceae)

ALSO KNOWN AS
Husk tomato, groundcherry, tomate verde, tomatillo pourpre

NATIVE RANGE
Mexico to Central America, Cuba to Haiti

NATURALIZED IN
Grows widely in suitable climates

GROWING CONDITIONS
An annual or short-lived perennial of the tropics and subtropics, where it is found at elevations up to 2,600 m (8,500 ft). Happy in full sun or partial shade in moist, free-draining soil, and can tolerate daytime temperatures of 8–31°C (46–88°F).

WHERE TO FIND
At farmers' markets and, increasingly, supermarkets worldwide.

HOW TO EAT
Use the fresh fruit (which is high in vitamins and minerals) in salads and as a garnish, or bake or roast it for use in salsas, soups and sauces.

A staple of Mexican cuisine for millennia, the tomatillo (Spanish for 'little tomato') remains relatively unknown as a fruit outside the Americas, although it will be familiar to lovers of Mexican food as an ingredient in soups and salsas. From its natural and historic home of Mexico, Guatemala and the southern United States, production and use are now established in India and growing in Australia. Readily accessible to those in colder climates as a canned product, it is finding its way into dishes beyond salsa verde and curry. And where the fresh fruit is unavailable, the plant is easily cultivated in much the same way as a tomato. Seedlings become typically ungainly plants with stems more than 1 metre (3 feet) long that need support; however, a useful adaptation allows any stems that touch the soil to root and ultimately form separate, cloned plants.

The genus *Physalis* is distinctive for its papery husk, a feature that is perhaps better known from the tomatillo's popular relative, the Cape gooseberry or goldenberry (*Physalis peruviana*), which is widely used as a decorative – not to mention tasty – garnish for desserts in restaurants. This husk, which is botanically the calyx, has evolved to encase the fruit, affording it some protection as it ripens, as demonstrated by the incredible 52-million-year-old tomatillo fossil that was found in Argentina in 2017. The common name of both tomatillo and tomato is derived from the Aztec word *tomatl*, signifying a watery, globose fruit containing many seeds.

Being a plant of arid regions, the tomatillo is adaptable to a wide range of nutritionally poor soils; it can also tolerate drought and even grow in saline conditions. The husk acts as natural packaging that extends the fruit's shelf life, making the tomatillo a great crop for dry-region farmers.

The fruit can be eaten raw or cooked. With a texture and flavour akin to a slightly unripe tomato, it is great in refreshingly sour drinks, as a garnish, in salads, soups, stews and sauces, or with grilled vegetables. Although ubiquitous, the Mexican salsa verde is justifiably popular; it is made by blending cooked tomatillos with chopped onion, coriander (cilantro), jalapeño chillies, salt and fresh lime juice.

Vallonea Oak

Quercus ithaburensis subsp. *macrolepis* (Fagaceae)

ALSO KNOWN AS
Camatina

NATIVE RANGE
Southeastern Italy, Balkan
Peninsula to Syria

GROWING CONDITIONS
Shallow, neutral soil in semi-arid
climates with warm winters,
in scrub and among mixed
deciduous trees up to an altitude
of 700 m (2,300 ft). For reliable
cropping, a Mediterranean
climate is required.

WHERE TO FIND
Fresh acorns can be foraged
throughout the growing range,
and acorn flour is increasingly
available from specialized online
food retailers.

HOW TO EAT
High in carbohydrates, vitamins
and minerals, acorns are useful
for soups, stews and vegetarian
burger patties or in powdered
form for jellies and various
(gluten-free) baked goods.
The fruit must be leached of its
tannins before it is eaten.

The genus *Quercus*, universally known as oak – of which there are about 500 species – is widespread throughout the northern hemisphere and south towards the equator. The neotropics, particularly southern Mexico, boasts the greatest diversity. Wherever they grow, these trees are much admired for their beauty and, in many cases, sheer majesty, but to ancient people they meant much more. They were idolized as symbols of strength and longevity, their timber used in the building of homes and ships or as fuel, their acorns a food for human and beast alike.

This last use was all but forgotten outside a handful of Indigenous cultures, and it was the American anthropologist Edward Winslow Gifford who in the early twentieth century recognized the oaks' largely historic importance as a source of food. Having dedicated his life to studying the Indigenous people of California, Gifford found the acorn to be a staple food of the past. As such, he is believed to be the originator of the term 'balanophagy', from the Greek roots *bálanos* (acorn) and *phageîn* (to eat) – essentially, the practice of eating acorns. Once the preserve of academia, this word is now used among growing numbers of commercial producers of acorns and their derivatives. For Gifford, *Q. agrifolia*, the Californian live oak, was the focus, but several oaks and their close relatives are used around the world. *Lithocarpus corneus*, for example, is favoured by Koreans, by far the biggest consumers of acorns.

Since 2015 an initiative on the Greek island of Kea has successfully revived the local acorn-based industry using *Q. ithaburensis* subsp. *macrolepis*, a species of vallonea oak that covers the island. This tree produces a large acorn weighing about 30 grams (1 ounce), the caps of which are removed and sold locally as a dye, or to leather tanneries, which value natural tannins over chemical alternatives. Once dried to the point of rattling in their shells, the acorns themselves are soaked repeatedly in hot or room-temperature water to remove the tannins. They are then shelled and coarsely ground, after which a

continues

final soak, drying and grinding into flour result in a product that is packaged and shipped internationally.

Perfectly adapted to the Mediterranean climate, the vallonea oak can grow in a wide range of soils and dry climates, stabilizing the soil with its extensive roots, braving strong winds and forming open, park-like woodlands. It is ideal for dry-region silvopasture systems, whereby grazing animals and tree crops are kept on the same land, resulting in a highly productive, resilient and biodiverse landscape. Unlike most other nut trees, the vallonea oak can produce a high yield without the need for human input, such as fertilizer or irrigation.

The fruit can be eaten once it is freed of tannins. A Korean acorn jelly called *dotori-muk* is made by grinding fresh acorns into a powder that is leached of its tannins in large vats. The powder is then dried and further pulverized before it is boiled in water until it reaches a pudding-like consistency. This pudding is served with thinly sliced chillies, carrots, lettuce and green onions before being seasoned with a mixture of soy sauce, sesame oil and seeds, garlic, chilli flakes and brown sugar. Leached acorns have a slightly dry texture akin to that of chestnuts, and a similarly nutty, sweet flavour, making them great for soups and stews, in vegetarian burger patties, or as a coffee substitute or even a liqueur. Acorn flour is useful in gluten-free baking and for making noodles.

Black Radish

Raphanus raphanistrum subsp. *sativus*
(syn. *Raphanus sativus* var. *niger*) (Brassicaceae)

ALSO KNOWN AS
Rettich, rábano de invierno,
luo bo, radis d'automne et d'hiver

NATIVE RANGE
Eastern Mediterranean

NATURALIZED IN
Widely in suitable climates

GROWING CONDITIONS
A cool-weather crop that grows in
a range of consistently moist soils
in full sun or partial shade. Good
air movement and drainage are
important to avoid fungal growth.

WHERE TO FIND
Farmers' markets throughout its
growing range.

HOW TO EAT
Use as you would any radish in
salads or salsas, or eat it roasted,
fried or sautéed. Try adding the
leaves to a stir-fry.

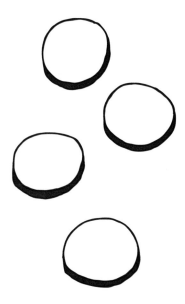

Nowadays any connoisseur of fine dining or home-grown vegetables is aware that, when it comes to the humble radish, there is much to discover beyond the pink globe and French breakfast varieties. Because it has been cultivated widely for millennia, there is much debate about the radish's origins. We will probably never know where it came from, because it is considered a cultigen: a plant that has been altered by humans through selective breeding. However, evidence does reveal two early centres of diversification: Central Asia and the Mediterranean.

Among the ancient cultivated varieties, it was the black radish that was most prevalent. Today this historic variety (correctly a subspecies) is enjoying a resurgence, and is desirable for its flavour and nutritional benefits, attributes that were well known in ancient Egypt, Greece and Rome. Perceived to have energy-boosting properties, black radish is believed to have been a staple food of pyramid builders between about 2550 and 2490 BCE. Radishes were valued so highly by the ancient Greeks that small replicas of them were made in gold; beetroot (beets), on the other hand, were cast in silver, and turnips in lead. In the rest of Europe radish consumption is recorded much later, firstly in thirteenth-century Germany and then in England in 1548. By the late sixteenth century radishes were being grown in North America and Mexico.

The black radish grows in a variety of consistently moist soils, its vigorous taproot offering a novel solution to the problem of soil compaction, and it is increasingly being grown once again throughout Europe and North America. If it is planted as an autumnal cover crop, its roots 'biodrill' deep into the earth, breaking up the water-impervious hardpan and blazing a trail for succeeding crops.

The bulbous taproot and leaves are both edible cooked or raw. Eaten raw, the root has a crunchy texture with a pungent, slightly earthy, bitter taste reminiscent of horseradish. Those flavours mellow considerably with cooking. Since most of the intense aromas are in the skin, it becomes milder when peeled. A classic Bavarian recipe, *Radisalat*, mixes coarsely grated, salted raw black radish with a dash of water, vinegar, oil and sugar. The root can also be tossed raw in salads, made into salsa, lacto-fermented or even juiced, or roasted, fried and sautéed. The milder-tasting fresh leaves are great in stir-fries.

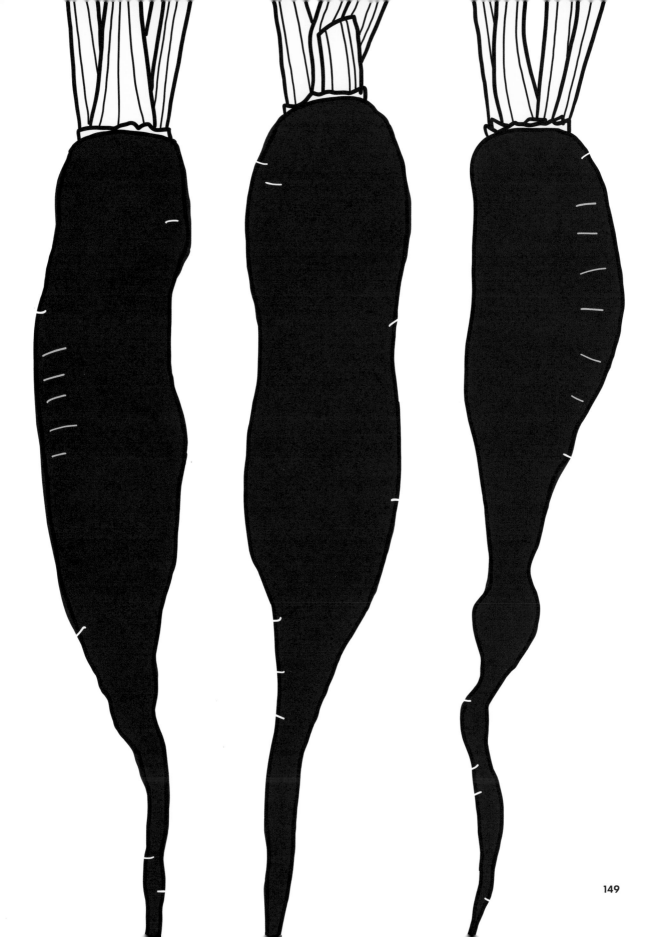

Cosconilla

Reichardia picroides (Asteraceae)

In the age of convenience and increasing availability of generic foods, traditional knowledge of 'wild edibles' is under pressure. However, at no other time has there been more interest in seeking out lost or scarce knowledge, and this task is often coordinated by ethnobotanists. Such dedication is exemplified in efforts focused on countries of the Mediterranean basin, to which cosconilla, *Reichardia picroides*, is native and where it was historically foraged as a wild plant.

In Italy *R. picroides* has enjoyed continuous use among rural communities and, as such, has many colloquial names. A member of the daisy family, it forms tight rosettes of long leaves varying from pale green to blue green with subtle or pronounced lobes and flowering stems up to 45 centimetres (18 inches) long, each bearing a bright, sunny yellow ray-floret. The plants have long taproots that, although they can be eaten, are secondary to the leaves, which are used in salads and celebrated as *ta chòrta*, wild edible greens. Naturally adapted to challenging conditions, including coastal salt, drought and inland heat, and growing vigorously on everything from dry, rocky soil to ancient monuments and even sand dunes, cosconilla is an immensely adaptable and productive plant that has potential commercially as a low-input, slug-proof salad crop of traditional and hydroponic farming.

The leaves, which are high in antioxidants, are edible cooked or raw, while the roots can be roasted and ground into a coffee substitute, in the same way as dandelion. In Italy the fresh leaves of *caccialepre*, as it is called there, are eaten raw as a salad, seasoned with olive oil, salt and a squeeze of lemon. They have a slightly fleshy, crunchy texture with a mild, pleasantly bittersweet taste that is enhanced by a certain saltiness when grown along the coast. They are also eaten boiled, as fillings for pies, in pasta or in egg-based dishes. Interestingly – and unusually – the mature leaves are tastier than the young ones.

ALSO KNOWN AS
French scorzonera, caccialepre, common brighteyes

NATIVE RANGE
The Mediterranean

NATURALIZED IN
Gulf States, Hawaii, Western Australia

GROWING CONDITIONS
Grows on a range of acid to alkaline sandy, loam and clay soils in full sun or partial shade. Adapted to exposed coastal habitats but also found on cultivated fields, path- and roadsides, disturbed land, woodland and rocky scrub. Tolerates temperatures as low as -10°C (14°F) in free-draining soil with few nutrients.

WHERE TO FIND
Available from foragers all around the Mediterranean, or as seeds to grow in the garden.

HOW TO EAT
Eat the leaves (high in antioxidants) fresh in salads or use in pies, pasta or egg-based dishes. The roots can be roasted and ground into a coffee substitute.

ALSO KNOWN AS
Luju, biba, Japanese medlar, néflier du Japon, Japanische Mispel, yenidünya

NATIVE RANGE
China

NATURALIZED IN
In regions of suitable climate

GROWING CONDITIONS
Grows in semi-subtropical climates on a range of soils. Requires a mild (maritime) climate for maximum fruiting.

WHERE TO FIND
Worldwide, as fresh fruit or products derived from it.

HOW TO EAT
Loquat fruit is rich in potassium and antioxidants. Enjoy it ripe as it is, eat it stuffed with minced lamb, or use it in jams, jellies, juice or wine.

Loquat

Rhaphiolepis bibas (Rosaceae)

The family Rosaceae gives a bounty of diverse fruit, including apples, almonds, apricots, plums, cherries, strawberries and, indeed, roses themselves. However, there is one among them that many people consider to be the most delicious of all: the loquat, *Rhaphiolepis bibas*, which is perfectly accessible as a garden fruit or supermarket purchase in countries with agreeable climates.

It all began more than 2,000 years ago as wild plants from Hubei province, China, entered cultivation. The sixteenth-century book *Flora sinensis* (Flora of China) by the Polish missionary Michał Boym is believed to be the first European record of the loquat. Since then, through ecological adaptation and deliberate selection, many cultivars have become available, initially from China and Japan, later from Mediterranean countries, and then from the United States.

There are a few limiting factors to the loquat's wider availability. It is unusual in its family for flowering in the autumn or early winter, and ripening its fruit in spring and early summer. This is a barrier to fruit ripening in colder climates, since, although established trees tolerate temperatures as low as -12°C (10°F), the flowers and fruit are sensitive to frost and need reasonably bright, dry conditions if they are to develop. This will always be the case, and will, it is to be hoped, alter only slowly with climate change. Perishability and vulnerability to mechanical damage are further obstacles, although a combination of cultivar selection, natural treatments (such as a coating of cinnamon oil), and improved machinery and logistics will allow the fresh fruit to become more widely available.

The adaptable loquat can grow in a wide range of soils. Being evergreen and very tolerant of pruning, it makes a productive living fence, one that also stabilizes the soil and provides ample nectar for pollinators.

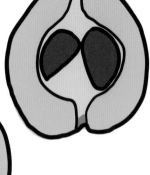

The fruit can be eaten both cooked and raw. With variable texture and a flavour somewhere between a crisp plum and a juicy apricot, it is perfect for jams, jellies, juices, wine, canning or even drying. A savoury Turkish recipe, *yenidünya kebabı*, is made by stuffing pitted loquats with spiced minced lamb before roasting them on the grill or in the oven.

Marsh Samphire

Salicornia europaea (Amaranthaceae)

Over the last century sea levels have risen globally, challenging coastline communities of all kinds to invest in costly defences, adapt, or in some cases abandon their homes and livelihoods. An inevitable consequence is more frequent destructive storm surges that push further inland, increasing soil salinity and therefore posing a problem for traditional land-based crops. In some situations plants have adapted to salty environments, and these are known as halophytes. A number are edible, such as those of the genus *Salicornia*, often collectively known as glassworts because of their traditional use in soda-based glass-making.

Glassworts are found in much of Eurasia, North America and South Africa, and among them is *S. europaea*, marsh samphire. Historically, cultures throughout its northern and western European range have enjoyed this highly nutritious vegetable in local dishes at a time when winter stores are depleted. Once the preserve of local foragers, it has been much publicized since the turn of the twenty-first century for its culinary delights, leading to greater demand and pressure on wild plants; in some cases, this has had to be regulated. Such demand has led to innovations in farmed production, sometimes in combination with marine aquaculture, since it is an effective bio-filter.

Growing where very few other plants dare to grow, marsh samphire is considered to be one of the most salt-tolerant plants in the world. By helping to stabilize coasts and estuaries, it can prevent shoreline erosion. It can also filter salt, heavy metals and nitrogen from contaminated water and soil both on the coast and inland. This makes it an ideal phytoremediation crop for restoring and protecting vulnerable ecosystems around the world, opening up numerous opportunities for regenerative agriculture.

Marsh samphire is high in vitamin A, minerals and fatty acids. Its shoots are edible cooked or raw, while its seeds are the source of a nutritious oil. In a simple French dish, *salicornes sautées en persillade*, blanched samphire is sautéed in butter with minced garlic, and finished with finely chopped parsley and ground black pepper. The crunchy, succulent shoots have a fresh, briny flavour that works well in salads, as a garnish for seafood, steamed, in soups and sauces, or pickled.

Surprising Plant Flavours

SWEET

SALTY

SOUR

BITTER

UMAMI

FATTY

There are six basic flavours that can be perceived by the taste buds on our tongue: sweet, salty, sour, bitter, umami (savoury) and even fatty (suggested by recent research). Already giving us a first impression of our food, it is the olfactory receptors of the nose that allow us to perceive more complex and nuanced flavours, such as vanilla, strawberry and chocolate. That is why everything tastes so bland when we have a cold and a blocked nose.

Working in unison, these two systems (together with trigeminal nerve stimulation, which allows us to register the texture and temperature of food) give us a complex picture of our daily food landscape. This allows us to perceive the sweet-and-sour crunchiness of a freshly picked apple, or the starchy sweetness with a hint of caramel from an oven-roasted sweet potato.

Yet these systems are also there to warn us of poisonous substances, such as ricin and cyanide. Particularly bitter notes trigger our primal early-warning system, but sour flavours are also on the watchlist. Having saved our ancestors countless times as they foraged for food, even today this stops us from eating spoiled food. Unfortunately, however, it also prevents us from eating many perfectly edible, even healthy plants, such as kale and other members of the brassica family, which produce bitter substances to deter animals from eating them and to ward off pests and disease. Most cultivars of edible plants that are commonly available today have been bred to reduce their bitterness and sourness, but a hint of these flavours will always remain.

So, what can you do to expand your edible plant repertoire if you aren't keen on bitter or sour flavours? Simply follow the method of countless coffee-drinkers. If you find a particular food too bitter, eat small amounts mixed with favourite vegetables, or add other ingredients to mask the taste. For instance, moderate amounts of umami-tasting soy sauce and/or natural sweeteners, such as maple syrup, are to broccoli what milk and sugar are to black coffee. Sour can be neutralized by various fats, as well as sweeteners.

Over time, slowly increase the 'dose' of the desired food until one day you have acquired the taste. In no time you will be able to enjoy a whole new world of healthy and delicious plant flavours. And if something really isn't for you, there are many other tasty edibles to try.

There are many fascinating edible plant flavours to discover, far beyond what is available in supermarkets:

- **SAFOU FRUIT**, with a buttery texture like that of an avocado, and a slightly sour, tangy flavour reminiscent of olives

- **LATÔ SEAWEED**, with a pleasurable pop when bitten into, and briny, slightly sweet-umami flavours

- The immature palm seeds of the **PALMYRA PALM**, with a jelly-like lychee texture and a refreshing flavour reminiscent of coconut

- The cooked young fronds of the **VEGETABLE FERN**, with a crunchy to slimy texture and a flavour reminiscent of asparagus, with a slightly tangy sweetness

- Cooked **KOCHIA** seeds, with a firm, crunchy texture on the outside, a creamy, buttery consistency on the inside and a light taste reminiscent of broccoli and artichoke

- The juicy fruit of **EBBING'S SILVERBERRY**, slightly tart, reminiscent of wild cherries and redcurrants.

Providing a multitude of exciting flavours, textures and aromas, these are only a few examples of plants that are already regional heroes and that have the potential to revolutionize the global flavour landscape.

Marula

Sclerocarya birrea (Anacardiaceae)

Food, medicine, culture and spirituality: a mosaic of African ethnobotanical heritage exists in one majestic tree, *Sclerocarya birrea*, widely known as marula. Its three subspecies cover vast areas of tropical Africa's drier regions, from Mauritania to Ethiopia, eastwards to the islands of Mayotte and Madagascar and down to South Africa. The discovery of 150,000-year-old archaeological deposits containing fragments of marula fruit seeds in what is now Zimbabwe suggests that this nutritious fruit helped to fuel the emerging dominance of *Homo sapiens*. So began humankind's long and mutually beneficial relationship with this botanical treasure, which has amassed a wealth of local names, customs and uses. Following pink flowers (1) and falling from the tree green (2) to ripen yellow (3), marula fruit is about the size of a plum. A single managed, wild or semi-wild mature tree can produce up to 500 kilograms (1,100 pounds) of fruit every year. Depending on the region, trees are shared among the community or owned by families and, as such, gain their protection and care. Anecdotes of elephants and other wild animals being found drunk after having feasted on fermenting windfalls go back centuries, but, although amusing, have been disproved in recent studies.

Withstanding some of sub-Saharan Africa's harshest conditions, the marula tree can grow on everything from nutritionally poor and rocky soils to those that are very salty. Growing fast and yielding huge amounts of fruit, it is already a vital source of food and income for many communities, and will be much more so in an unsteady future shaped by climate change.

The fruit and kernel (4) can be eaten cooked or raw. The ripe fruit has a leathery skin and juicy pulp with a sweet, nutty, slightly tart flavour; it is perfect for jams, jellies, juices, ciders, chutneys, pie fillings and, most famously, Amarula cream liqueur. The nut, which tastes a little like macadamia, is eaten raw, toasted, as nut butter, ground into a gluten-free flour or added to soup, and is the source of a valued edible oil. The much-loved Eswatinian alcoholic drink *buganu* is made by fermenting peeled, mashed marula fruit with water and sugar.

ALSO KNOWN AS
Morula, mufula, jelly plum, cat thorn, cider tree, maroola

NATIVE RANGE
Mauritania to Ethiopia, eastwards to the islands of Mayotte and Madagascar, and down to South Africa

NATURALIZED IN
Australia, India, Israel and the Sultanate of Oman

GROWING CONDITIONS
Wooded grassland, woodland and bushland, on rocky hills and sandy soil or occasionally sandy loam that is mildly acid to neutral and typically low in nutrients.

WHERE TO FIND
The fresh fruit is available at markets throughout sub-Saharan Africa, while various processed foods (such as oil and liqueur) are available worldwide through specialized food retailers.

HOW TO EAT
Enjoy the juicy fruit as it comes, or in jam, jelly or beer. The kernel is great raw, toasted, as nut butter or as gluten-free flour.

Heirloom Potatoes

Solanum tuberosum (Solanaceae)

ALSO KNOWN AS
Spud, papa, Kartoffel, patate, batata, viazi, kentang

NATIVE RANGE
Northwestern and southern Argentina, Bolivia, Chile, Peru, Colombia, Ecuador and Venezuela

NATURALIZED IN
In suitable climates

GROWING CONDITIONS
Requires an open, frost-free site in deep, fertile, moist, free-draining soil that is ideally neutral to slightly acid; tolerates some alkalinity.

WHERE TO FIND
At markets worldwide.

HOW TO EAT
Enjoy the famous tuber (rich in carbohydrates and minerals) cooked in a host of dishes, from soups to baked goods and even plant-based milks.

The potato – the world's fifth most important food crop, after sugar cane, maize, rice and wheat – is set to climb the rankings further. Capable of bigger yields than cereals on the same amount of land and in less time, this humble vegetable has a place in securing food security for developing countries. To achieve this, a concerted effort is underway to mitigate against a host of diseases, chief of which are the fungal pathogens that cause early and late potato blight. It was the latter that brought about the devastating Irish Great Famine of 1845–52, and since then, many innovations have reduced the threat, such as the use of 'clean' stock from in-vitro tissue-culture laboratories – a luxury not afforded to poorer countries.

The potato was first domesticated from wild plants in the Andes Mountains of South America some 10,000 years ago, and today there are thought to be more than 3,000 varieties in the region. Potatoes arrived in Europe a mere five centuries ago and were quickly established as a staple crop. Focus settled on ease of production and greater yield, and little attempt was made to move beyond favourite cultivars, which spread far and wide through colonialism. Despite this, and the ability of potatoes to be grown in climates as diverse as those of Russia and Rwanda, many countries developed their own varieties, of which some are considered heirloom. Experiencing something of a revival in recent years, heirloom varieties benefit local growers, add culinary versatility and secure genetics for future breeding.

Facing considerable challenges from climate change and a narrow genetic base, today's most common potato cultivars are in urgent need of becoming less resistant to change. They must adapt to heat, drought, pests, disease, heavy rain and waterlogging, all the while growing faster and maturing earlier. By going back to the beginning and using the genetics of wild species, cultigens and heirloom varieties, the scientific community and experts in the field can reduce such risks and, in the process, create or identify a range of varieties based on flavour, nutrients and climate. Heirloom varieties, being perfectly adapted to a wide range of soils and climates, hold the genetic key to a resilient future based not on a select few varieties that are grown globally, but rather on a rich diversity of regionally grown heirloom varieties.

This famous tuber must be eaten cooked. A hearty Peruvian street food, *papas rellenas*, consists of mashed potato dough shaped into a ball and stuffed with various fillings, such as minced (ground) beef, and deep-fried. Although the texture and flavour

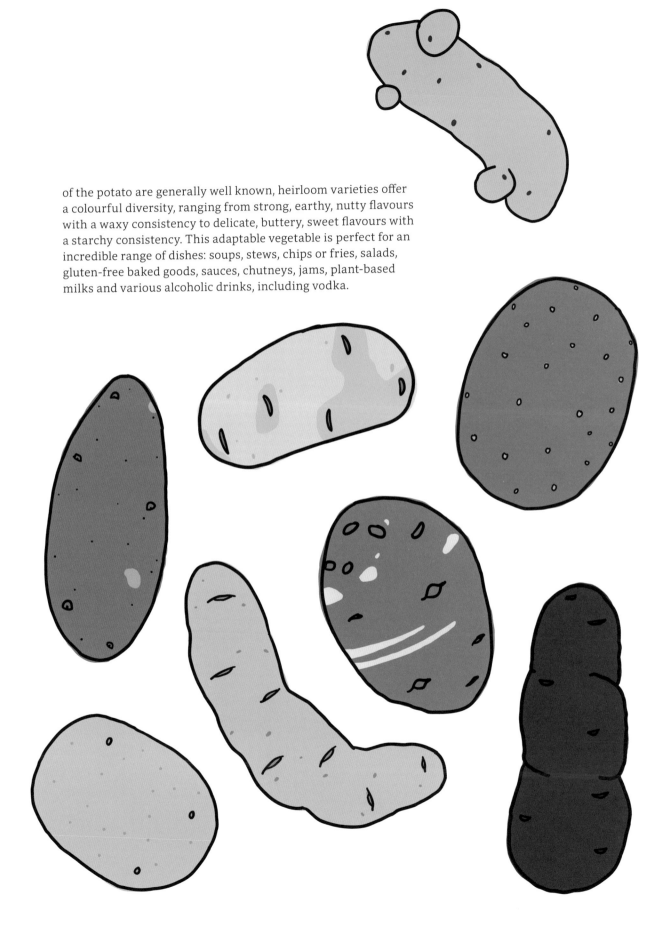

of the potato are generally well known, heirloom varieties offer
a colourful diversity, ranging from strong, earthy, nutty flavours
with a waxy consistency to delicate, buttery, sweet flavours with
a starchy consistency. This adaptable vegetable is perfect for an
incredible range of dishes: soups, stews, chips or fries, salads,
gluten-free baked goods, sauces, chutneys, jams, plant-based
milks and various alcoholic drinks, including vodka.

Tamarind

Tamarindus indica (Fabaceae)

ALSO KNOWN AS
Indian date

NATIVE RANGE
Madagascar and the
Comoros archipelago

NATURALIZED IN
Tropical Asia, the Arabian
Peninsula, tropical America,
the Caribbean, Australia and
many islands of the Pacific
and Indian oceans

GROWING CONDITIONS
Dry and semi-arid savanna and
bushland; can also be found
growing in valleys, alongside
streams, ponds and rivers.

WHERE TO FIND
Fresh tamarind is available at
markets throughout its growing
region, while various products
(such as paste, drinks and dried
pulp) are available worldwide.

HOW TO EAT
Use the antioxidant-rich pulp in
refreshing sweet-and-sour drinks,
chutneys and curries. The flowers
and leaves are an excellent
vegetable, while the ground seeds
provide a gluten-free flour.

The mighty tamarind tree, *Tamarindus indica*, is a sight to behold. It stands up to 30 metres (100 feet) tall and has a dense, spreading crown as wide as 12 metres (40 feet) clad in evergreen, acacia-like foliage, with numerous leaflets that fold and close at night. The fragrant, orchid-like flowers have three creamy petals patterned with red veins, as well as two tiny thread-like petals that are barely visible. Borne in summer on short inflorescences, they are followed by plump cinnamon-brown seedpods 15 centimetres (6 inches) long, indicative of the legume family, to which tamarind belongs.

Ancient demand for tamarind's fruit and hard-wearing red timber expanded the tree's prehistoric distribution, but after some botanical detective work Madagascar has been identified as its probable origin. On encountering it in western India, Arab sea-traders thought its sticky black pulp and seeds resembled those of their native date palm, so 'tamarind' was born of the Arabic for date palm (*tamr*) and for India (*hind*). Recorded cultivation dates from the fourth century BCE in the eastern Mediterranean.

Despite being common throughout the tropics, tamarind is at risk in Madagascar, as forests are burned for charcoal or cleared for cereals and pasture. Mature tamarind trees deter the germination of their own, their relatives' and other species' seeds beneath their canopies using naturally occurring allelochemicals, an evolutionary mechanism to limit competition for light and resources. Tamarind is a key food of the ring-tailed lemur, which aids in its seed dispersal, and a lack of non-related trees means the tamarind cannot colonize new territory because its seeds are defecated only beneath its own branches. This jeopardizes the whole ecosystem, creating isolated groups of both tamarind and lemur, and disrupting the biodiversity to which they are integral.

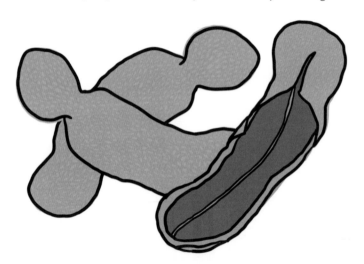

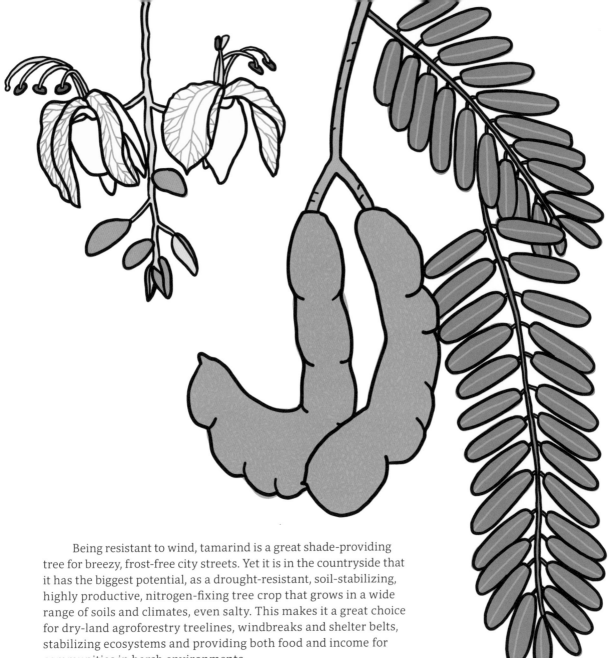

Being resistant to wind, tamarind is a great shade-providing tree for breezy, frost-free city streets. Yet it is in the countryside that it has the biggest potential, as a drought-resistant, soil-stabilizing, highly productive, nitrogen-fixing tree crop that grows in a wide range of soils and climates, even salty. This makes it a great choice for dry-land agroforestry treelines, windbreaks and shelter belts, stabilizing ecosystems and providing both food and income for communities in harsh environments.

The young leaves, flowers and fleshy pulp of the seedpod can be eaten cooked or raw, but the seed and mature leaves must be cooked. A refreshing chilled Turkish summer drink, *demirhindi şerbeti*, is made by soaking and simmering peeled tamarind seedpods before adding cardamom, nutmeg, ginger, cinnamon and sugar. With a date-like texture and a sweet, sour flavour reminiscent of citrus and caramel, the ripe fruit pulp is perfect for jams, juices, curries, chutneys, sauces, soft drinks and wines. Once soaked, boiled and freed of their coating, the seeds can be eaten roasted or ground into a powder and used as a stabilizer, thickening agent or gluten-free flour. The leaves and flowers are used as a sour vegetable in chutneys, curries, chillies and pickles.

Dandelion

Taraxacum officinale (Asteraceae)

Like their seed on the breeze, opinions and emotions evoked by the humble dandelion have come and gone throughout history. Of the 2,500 or so species, found mainly in the warmer temperate zones of the northern hemisphere, there is no doubt that *Taraxacum officinale* is the best-known and most studied. These are among the very few garden flowers that children can pick without permission, and, of course, their amazing fluffy, translucent, spherical seed heads provide no end of pleasure. Among the pastimes they inspire is making a wish upon blowing free their fine, feathery filaments. However, despite these fond memories, many people grow up to see dandelions as weeds, unwelcome in highly manicured lawns, their image often featured on the labels of noxious herbicides.

Such negative perception is comparatively new. Throughout history dandelions have been cherished for their medicinal and edible uses by such ancient cultures as the Chinese, Egyptians and Romans. Indeed, the Latin name *Taraxacum* is from the Greek *taraxos* (disorder) and *akos* (cure). Along with other *Taraxacum* species favoured for their culinary use, the common dandelion is easily accessible as a foraged, garden or window-box crop and should be considered on a par with more common salad crops.

Being a highly robust, fast-growing plant, the dandelion has an extremely bright future, both on this world and off it. On this planet, its deep-reaching, powerful taproot loosens hard-packed soil, while the whole plant can rehabilitate soil that is polluted with heavy metal (rendering the plant inedible, of course). Off the Earth, experiments have shown it to grow very well in simulated Martian soil, making it an ideal, highly nutritious food crop for future space missions.

All parts of the dandelion are edible cooked or raw. The young leaves have a fresh, crunchy consistency and a pleasant bittersweet flavour; they become increasingly bitter as they mature. The leaves taste great in salads, smoothies, soups, sauces, stir-fries, omelettes and drinks. A favourite Austrian spring recipe, *Röhrlsalat*, is made by mixing coarsely chopped new dandelion leaves with sliced boiled potatoes and marinating in pumpkin-seed oil, apple cider vinegar, mustard and salt. Dandelion flower buds can be pickled like capers, while the open flowers can be eaten in salads, made into tasty fritters, syrups, teas, beers or soft drinks, or used as a beautiful garnish. Even the peeled taproot can be eaten much as parsnips are, and, if roasted, makes a substitute for coffee.

ALSO KNOWN AS
Faceclock, blowball, løvetand, Löwenzahn, diente di león, paardenbloem

NATIVE RANGE
Europe and Asia

NATURALIZED IN
Worldwide

GROWING CONDITIONS
Common in grassland and cultivated ground in temperate climates, where it prefers rich, moist, free-draining soils of light acidity to light alkalinity in full sun or partial shade. Adaptable to both light, sandy soils and those of heavy clay and high alkalinity, and tolerates maritime exposure. In tropical climates, it can be grown in the shade as a seasonal vegetable.

WHERE TO FIND
Fresh leaves are increasingly available at markets worldwide or can be foraged from unpolluted fields, meadows or lawns. Dandelion-root coffee is available from specialized retailers worldwide.

HOW TO EAT
Enjoy the young leaves (a good source of vitamins and minerals) in salads, stir-fries and omelettes, or simply sautéed. The open flower makes a delicious tea, while the peeled roots can be eaten much like parsnips.

Prekese

Tetrapleura tetraptera (Fabaceae)

ALSO KNOWN AS
Aridan, gum tree, kikangabalimu, uhio, ighimiakia, ikoho, ebuk

NATIVE RANGE
Western tropical Africa to Kenya and Angola

GROWING CONDITIONS
Found in secondary forest, preferring the fringes of lowland rainforests. Also found in southern savanna-woodland and forest outliers in the African plains. Tolerates a range of soils but prefers mildly acidic loamy sand. Seedlings require the full shade of surrounding trees before acclimatizing to full sun.

WHERE TO FIND
At markets throughout its growing regions, or worldwide from specialized online retailers.

HOW TO EAT
Use as an aromatic spice (a good source of minerals) in soups, stews, sauces, soft drinks, teas and clear spirits.

Prekese, 'soup perfume' in the Twi dialect of Ghana, is just one of many colloquial names attributed to *Tetrapleura tetraptera*, a medium-sized deciduous tree of the bean family native to parts of Africa. The ethnomedicinal/botanical uses of this cherished tree are many and varied. Its anti-inflammatory properties are used to treat such conditions as arthritis, rheumatism and high cholesterol, while consuming the fruit, or spices derived from it, helps to repel mosquitoes, which – unlike humans – don't care for it. Other regional names reflect mystical properties. *Aridan* in the Yoruba dialect of Nigeria means 'cast no spell', and *kikangabalimu* 'it scares ghosts' in the Rwamba dialect of Uganda. Flowers – creamy-pink maturing to orange crowd short spikes – towards the end of February are followed by dark purple-brown, slightly curved pod-like fruit up to 25 centimetres (10 inches) long, ripening from September to December. Two of the pod's four distinct longitudinal wings contain soft, sugary, aromatic pulp as an incentive to seed-dispersing megafauna, nowadays the African forest elephant. Deforestation and poaching have sent both into decline, their fates inextricably linked, and both are reliant on local initiatives to counter and repair the damage of recent generations.

Growing in a wide range of soils in semi-deciduous woodland of the tropical lowlands, prekese is a drought-resistant tree that has considerable potential as a valuable spice crop with a long shelf life in dry-land agroforestry systems. It has the capacity to be a valuable source of income for subsistence farmers in sub-Saharan Africa and beyond.

The fruit pod is used as a spice. A traditional Ghanaian and Nigerian soup known as *banga* is made by cooking various meats and fish with onions, peppers, bitter leaves, ginger, tomatoes and palm-nut extract, flavoured with prekese and other spices just before serving. The pod has a highly fragrant, sugary aroma with slightly savoury-astringent notes that add to any soup, stew, cooked meat, soda, syrup, sweet or tea. It is also used to flavour clear spirits.

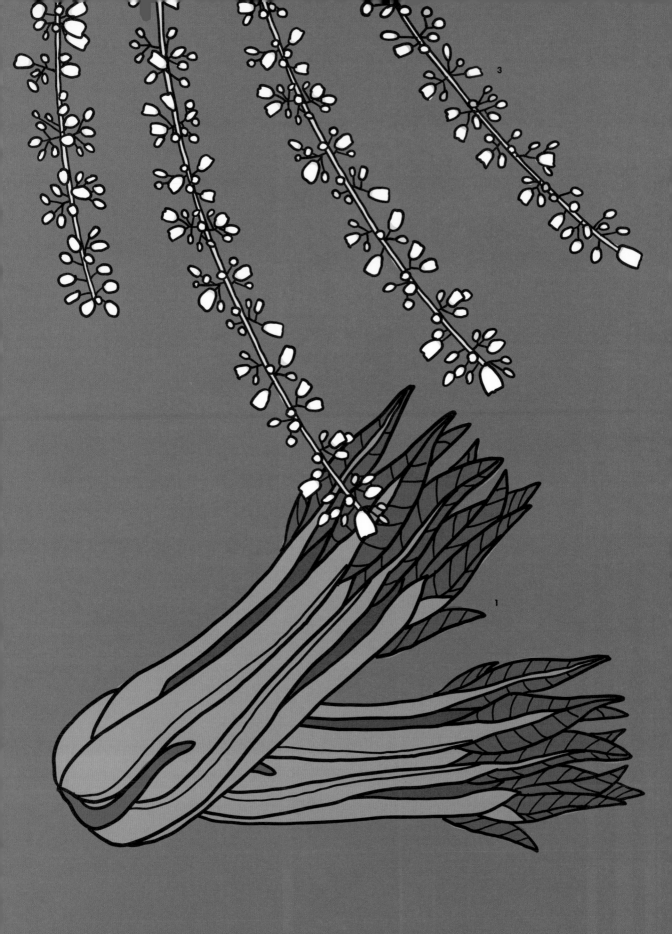

Chinese Toon

Toona sinensis (Meliaceae)

Xiāngchūn ('fragrant spring'), more commonly known as Chinese toon, has been enjoyed as a seasonal vegetable and medicinal herb in northern China since antiquity. The tender new shoots **(1)** of this tree, being high in vitamins and antioxidants, are traditionally enjoyed in late April and early May as a tonic to strengthen the immune system after winter. As such, the tree is integral to the Gu Yu ('Grain Rain') festival, the sixth of the Chinese lunar calendar's twenty-four solar terms: peak time for planting rice and corn, and for the growth of cotton.

In 2019 Chinese toon became the unlikely subject of self-fulfilling media interest as local reports of its increasing price meant that it momentarily reached parity with lobster and other luxury foods. That gave rise to the term *'xiāngchūn* freedom' to describe those wealthy enough to afford such luxury. Having been picked up by the international press, Chinese toon is now

continues

continues

2

ALSO KNOWN AS
Chinese cedar, red toon, Chinese mahogany, xiāngchūn

NATIVE RANGE
Indian subcontinent to central and southern China and western Malesia

NATURALIZED IN
Tanzania, Uganda, Afghanistan, Korea and Maryland (USA)

GROWING CONDITIONS
Grows in moderately humid to humid subtropical and mid- to high-elevation tropical climates in forests, steep hillsides, ravines and near waterways in full sun or partial shade on a range of moist, well-drained soils. Spring growth is vulnerable to frost, but once established, woody growth can tolerate lows of around -25°C (-13°F). Germinates readily in accommodating situations and climates, where it can become invasive, aided by suckering growth.

WHERE TO FIND
At markets throughout China and Malaysia.

HOW TO EAT
Enjoy the tender young shoots (rich in vitamin B) and leaves in salads, soups, stir-fries and egg-based dishes.

drawing greater attention as a vegetable with home-grown and commercial prospects beyond its native range. It is widely grown as an ornamental, most notably in cool temperate countries, where it is celebrated as the hardiest member of the mahogany family (followed closely by the Indian bead tree, *Melia azedarach*). Asian culinary fame has inspired Western foodies to seek out local trees and taste the new growth for themselves, sometimes to the bemusement of garden-centre staff and professional gardeners. In the variety 'Flamingo' spring growth is vivid pink (2), which, along with summer heads of white–pink flowers (3) followed by fruit (4), makes it a great-value garden edible. Pruning the main trunk to limit its height not only makes the shoots accessible but also encourages more suckering.

A very fast-growing tree that is resistant to frost and disease, Chinese toon is simultaneously a culinary delight and a great timber tree for fine furniture. This is a rare combination that makes it an ideal crop for agroforestry farmers both looking for an early return on investment, by harvesting a portion of its highly sought-after spring foliage every year, and keen to nurture a valuable long-term investment in the form of high-quality timber. In particular, the savoury, slightly beef-like flavour of the young foliage promises exciting all-natural flavouring opportunities in the rapidly growing field of plant-based 'meats'.

The young shoots and leaves (5) are eaten cooked. The shoots have a pleasantly crispy texture and an unusual savoury flavour reminiscent of beef and some mushrooms. They are perfect for salads, soups, stir-fries, egg-based dishes and pickles, steamed, or as a dry or paste-based seasoning. They can also be infused into tea. A favourite Chinese recipe, peanut and toon salad (6), consists of blanched and coarsely chopped Chinese toon shoots and freshly roasted peanuts, dressed with black vinegar, olive oil, minced garlic, red chilli and a little sugar.

6

5

4

Food as Medicine

'Let food be thy medicine and medicine be thy food' is a maxim often ascribed to the ancient Greek physician Hippocrates. Whether or not he actually said it, nutrition is today – and in many cultures has been for millennia – considered a critical part of health, and is given a key role in the prevention and treatment of disease. Directly linked to a stronger immune system, safer pregnancies and childbirth, a lower risk of non-communicable disease (such as diabetes and cardiovascular disease) and overall longer life, good nutrition is widely considered to be the foundation of good health. It can even act as a form of medicine, and help in the management or reversal of disease processes.

The reasons for this are complex and not yet fully understood in scientific terms. There is, however, increasing evidence that a key role seems to fall to the gut microbiome, the community of trillions of bacteria, protozoa, viruses and fungi living in our intestines. Considerably outnumbering the body's total number of human cells, it is comprised of thousands of different species that fulfil a number of important functions, chiefly helping with digestion and controlling the immune and central nervous systems. While most of these organisms seem to be extremely important for our health, some can influence it negatively.

Although there is still no consensus among scientists as to what exactly constitutes a healthy gut microbiome, several recent studies point towards species diversity as a positive indicator. Besides family genes, environment and medication use, this diversity seems to be linked to the variety of food eaten, in particular minimally processed plant foods. This resonates strongly with the global focus on a plant-based diet as the solution to many environmental problems. Consisting primarily of fruit, vegetables, nuts, seeds, wholegrains and legumes, as well as – if desired – moderate amounts of animal-based products, such as meat, eggs and dairy, this is now widely considered to be the healthiest choice as well as the most environmentally responsible.

Yet it is not only the diversity of food that seems to be of importance to our health, but also its quality. For plants to provide all essential nutrients, vitamins and antioxidants, they must themselves be grown in healthy ecosystems with fertile soil. It is a beautiful link, considering that we can create the thriving ecosystems that in turn produce food that nourishes our health.

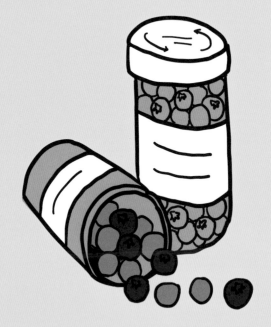

Water Caltrop

Trapa natans (Lythraceae)

ALSO KNOWN AS
Water nut, water chestnut, buffalo nut, bat nut, devil pod, Jesuit nut, ling nut, moustache nut, singhara, horn chestnut

NATIVE RANGE
Spain and Sweden (now extinct in both countries), Eurasia and northwestern Africa

NATURALIZED IN
United States and Canada

GROWING CONDITIONS
Most abundant in warm temperate freshwater ecosystems in quiet water bodies of variable depths. Typically annual, but can be perennial in tropical and subtropical regions.

WHERE TO FIND
At markets throughout Asia; can be foraged from unpolluted water in North America.

HOW TO EAT
Eat the carbohydrate-rich seed cooked and lightly salted as a snack, in stir-fries, as a dumpling filling or even candied. Dried and ground, it can be used as a gluten-free flour.

Ever present, lost, found, edible, inedible, eco menace, eco saviour, Jesuit nut or devil pod: few plants have amassed such a fascinating history and so many conflicting perceptions as water caltrop, *Trapa natans*. Despite being referred to commonly as water chestnut, it is a very different plant – and, indeed, food – from its namesake of Chinese restaurant fame, which comes from the underground corm of *Eleocharis dulcis*. Unlike any other fruit, that of *T. natans* is shaped like the caltrop, an ancient instrument of war in the form of a spiked tetrahedron.

Water caltrop is an aquatic plant with submerged stems extending up to 5 metres (17 feet) and carrying very fine photosynthesizing roots that allow the plant to grow in, and indeed clean up, polluted water. The toothed, triangular leaves form floating rosettes **(1)** anchored in the sediment beneath, while inflated leaf stalks provide buoyancy. Small white flowers are followed by the distinctive fruit **(2)**, which is dispersed by simply floating off or hitching a ride on a passing animal.

Throughout its native range, water caltrop is considered an important historic and/or current food source. There are archaeological and cultural references aplenty; its remains dating from 4,200 BCE have been found among waterlogged dwellings of Cham-Eslen on Lake Zug, Switzerland. A novel harvesting technique was developed in Turkey, where people living beside the Black Sea knew the fruit as *chilim* (from the Turkish for rug); with stones attached for ballast, these carpets were sunk beneath dense stands of *Trapa* and, after a time, raised, bringing forth a great bounty.

An effective colonizer that is easily harnessed for production in paddy fields, water caltrop is conversely seen as nothing more than a pernicious weed in parts of North America and elsewhere. But, being a fast-growing and high-yielding freshwater plant, it should be seen as a fascinating crop with immense potential.

2

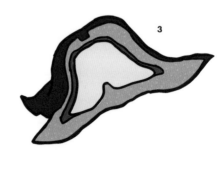

3

1

It can absorb vast amounts of nitrogen from shallow water, reducing the potential for the suffocation of the water through the explosive growth of phytoplankton from too many nutrients – a phenomenon known as eutrophication. After it has absorbed all these extra nutrients, harvesting its biomass, including its large, nutritious seed (which is high in carbohydrates, fibre and protein), provides a feast and makes sure the nutrients stay out of the water. It is rare that an environmental problem can be solved through harvesting.

The peculiarly shaped seed **(3)** of water caltrop can be eaten cooked. It is sold simply roasted by Taiwanese street vendors, and its crunchy texture paired with its curious flavour combination of roasted chestnut and boiled potato make it great as a snack, in stir-fries, as a dumpling filling, candied as a sweet, or ground into a gluten-free flour and used in baking.

1   2   3

Moth Bean

Vigna aconitifolia (Fabaceae)

Vigna aconitifolia is an ancient legume of great practical and cultural importance throughout its native range. Commonly known as moth bean, from its Hindi name (pronounced 'moath', 'mat' or 'mote'), it has for millennia been an indispensable dietary staple of countryside and city alike. Not only do both bean and pod feature in many dishes, but also the plant provides livestock fodder and a green manure in what is often barren soil, depleted of nutrients. Farmers consider moth bean the most drought-resistant pulse crop for hot, arid to semi-arid regions, where it will crop on as little as 60 millimetres (less than 2½ inches) of annual rainfall. The first written reference to moth bean is found in *Taittirīya Brāhmaṇa*, a collection of sacred texts more than 2,400 years old, considered a commentary on the much older Yajurveda, 'worship knowledge'. An annual, scrambling ground cover of the legume family, it has small, bright yellow flowers **(1)** followed by pods about 4 centimetres (1½ inches) long **(2)**, containing about six seeds **(3)**, which are harvested from September to December.

Prospering in harsh dry-land habitats with little to no human input, the moth bean is a great source of protein for subsistence farming communities on nutrient-poor, marginal land. Its ability to fix nitrogen helps to improve soil conditions, while its fast-growing roots stabilize the land. Furthermore, its small genome makes it a promising contender for the role of model plant, to help scientists understand what makes plants highly resilient to extreme environments. Such knowledge is crucial for breeding resilient crops.

The green pods, seeds and sprouts of the moth bean must be cooked or ground into flour. The bean has a rich, nutty, slightly earthy flavour and is used whole or sprouted in curries, salads, stir-fries, pastes and dals. The flour is used in baking, and the cooked green pods are consumed as a vegetable. A favourite Indian snack, *Bikaneri bhujia*, is made with a dough of moth-bean and gram flour, as well as spices including chilli, black pepper, cardamom, cloves and salt, pressed through a sieve (strainer) and deep-fried in vegetable oil.

ALSO KNOWN AS
Mat bean, math, matki, dew bean, dew gram, Turkish gram, Mattenbohne

NATIVE RANGE
Southern and central China, India, Pakistan, Sri Lanka and Myanmar

NATURALIZED IN
Eritrea, Yemen

GROWING CONDITIONS
Grows on a range of acid and alkaline soils, preferring those of a light, sandy structure; tolerates mild maritime conditions, but dislikes waterlogging. Full sun and low-moderate to low rainfall between 24 and 32°C (75–90°F), although it tolerates higher temperatures.

WHERE TO FIND
Through specialized Indian food retailers worldwide.

HOW TO EAT
Enjoy the nutritious sprouted seeds (a great source of protein) in dals, curries, salads or pastes, or use the flour in baking.

Bambara Groundnut

Vigna subterranea (Fabaceae)

ALSO KNOWN AS
Bambara, Bambara bean,
hog peanut, Congo groundnut,
earth pea, njugo bean,
Congo earth pea, Madagascar
groundnut, stone groundnut

NATIVE RANGE
Cameroon, Central African
Republic, Chad, Nigeria
and Sudan

NATURALIZED IN
Africa more widely (including
Madagascar), India, Java and
Dominican Republic

GROWING CONDITIONS
Thrives in dry, marginal,
typically sandy soil at altitudes
of up to 2000 m (6,600 feet).
Tolerant of drought, frost and
high temperatures, but yield is
higher in moist soil and daytime
temperatures of 30–35°C
(86–95°F). For the best harvest,
plant in sandy loam that is rich in
organic matter. Prefers full sun,
but tolerates light shade.

WHERE TO FIND
Markets and African grocery
stores in Africa, Australia, Europe,
the Americas and Southeast Asia.

HOW TO EAT
The protein-rich seeds can be
enjoyed fresh, cooked or ground
into flour.

2

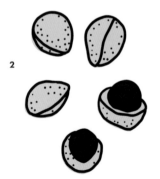

Grown throughout sub-Saharan Africa, the Bambara groundnut, *Vigna subterranea*, is at first glance unremarkable, a low-growing annual with no obvious attributes. But this humble legume is being promoted as a plant-based protein of the future. Such a confident prediction is built on years of work locally and internationally by experts in many disciplines. One might expect agronomists and nutritionists to be involved, but not necessarily anthropologists and sociologists. Experts in the former areas identified the Bambara groundnut (more accurately a seed or bean) as a 'complete food' of international appeal, while those in the latter groups were intrigued as to why its local potential was largely neglected. Grown alongside maize, millet, sorghum and cassava, the Bambara groundnut has been considered of less value, simply a back-up to mitigate against poor harvests of more important crops. A barrier to wider uptake was found to be based on several sociocultural practices with strict rules linked to fertility, healing and protection.

This is not unusual, since throughout history plants – especially the most useful ones – have been woven into local folklore and beliefs. In this case, East African people often refer to the Bambara groundnut as a 'woman's' crop, in the belief that it brings death to the household, and that only a mother who has lost a child can cultivate the plant and prepare the bean, being protected from further loss. It is now seen as both a local nutritious food and a valuable export opportunity, and researchers are building on the plant's nitrogen-fixing habit, and its ability to thrive in hot, semi-arid conditions and poor soil, by breeding and selecting high-yielding varieties. The attractive yellow flowers are hidden among the foliage at ground level, and once pollinated the developing fruit is drawn down into the soil (1), in an evolved defence against insects, which can devastate other crops, such as soybean.

A fast-growing year-round crop for tropical and subtropical climates, and a summer-season crop in Mediterranean climates, the Bambara groundnut is a promising future staple and is now increasingly being grown commercially. Being high-yielding, even in the worst of soils, and resistant to both drought and heavy rainfall, it is well equipped to deal with the extreme weather events brought about by climate change. Add to this its high protein content, its ability to improve poor soil and its independence of such agricultural input as fertilizer and one can't help wondering why it isn't already in widespread use.

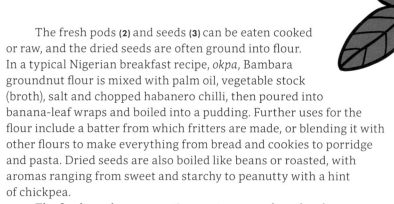

The fresh pods **(2)** and seeds **(3)** can be eaten cooked or raw, and the dried seeds are often ground into flour. In a typical Nigerian breakfast recipe, *okpa*, Bambara groundnut flour is mixed with palm oil, vegetable stock (broth), salt and chopped habanero chilli, then poured into banana-leaf wraps and boiled into a pudding. Further uses for the flour include a batter from which fritters are made, or blending it with other flours to make everything from bread and cookies to porridge and pasta. Dried seeds are also boiled like beans or roasted, with aromas ranging from sweet and starchy to peanutty with a hint of chickpea.

The fresh seeds are sometimes eaten raw, when they have a starchy, dry, peanut-like flavour. More often, the fresh pods are boiled with salt, resulting in a soft texture and a taste somewhere between that of peanuts and white beans.

Fox Grape

Vitis labrusca (Vitaceae)

ALSO KNOWN AS
Northern fox grape, labruscan
vineyard grape

NATIVE RANGE
Southeastern Canada to
eastern United States

NATURALIZED IN
Southern and central Europe,
Madeira, Azores, western
Russia, Tajikistan, Turkmenistan,
Ukraine, Uzbekistan, Vietnam,
Illinois (USA)

GROWING CONDITIONS
Tolerates a wide range of
soils (except waterlogged),
preferring those that are deep,
loamy, humus-rich and moist
but well drained.

WHERE TO FIND
Readily available throughout
North America; found at
farmers' markets and from
growers in Europe.

HOW TO EAT
The fresh fruit is high in
antioxidants. Enjoy it as a garnish,
or in jams, jellies, juices, ice
creams, pie fillings and wine.
The cooked young leaves can be
used as a vegetable, while the oil
made from the seeds can be used
for cooking.

Grapes have been cultivated for thousands of years, the majority for wine production. Most people presume this practice to have originated in Italy and Greece, but recent evidence takes us eastwards, to Georgia. This ancient intersection of Europe and Asia has revealed evidence of viticulture dating back some 8,000 years. From there, south and northwestwards, the native species *Vitis vinifera* went on to dominate international winemaking, bringing us such favourite grapes as Cabernet Sauvignon, Pinot Noir and Chardonnay.

Despite the continent being home to about twenty-five of the world's seventy-eight grape species, among them *V. labrusca*, the 'common vine', *V. vinifera*, was adopted by colonial North American producers in the mid-sixteenth century. But before this, the first Europeans to explore North America were Vikings from Greenland, who called it Vinland in what many believe to be a reference to the abundance of wild vines. Some Indigenous Americans produced a form of weak wine at this time, along with other fermented drinks. European colonists at first failed to establish imported varieties, which suffered from native pests and diseases. Progress was eventually made in the Spanish kingdoms of Las Californias and Santa Fe de Nuevo México, the foundations of today's Californian and New Mexican wine industry.

For decades connoisseurs dismissed native American grapes, and their flavours were even described as akin to 'animal fur and candied fruits'. The unfortunate fur reference has long persisted and features in one of the common names of *V. labrusca*: fox grape. Formerly, many considered fox grape nothing more than a rootstock for grafted *vinifera* varieties. Today, however, it and other native vines are seen as a genetic resource of untapped flavours and qualities that scientists and breeders can harness using DNA analysis and hybridizing techniques.

Tolerating a wide range of climatic and soil conditions, fox grapes, in times of ever-intensifying climate change, increasingly have the upper hand over more sensitive traditional cultivars. This makes them a great choice for cross-breeding, resulting in novel varieties that not only introduce resilience and diversity into existing vineyards but also unlock new winegrowing regions with traditionally unfavourable climates. Offering fantastically intense aromas and colours, they might just be the base for an exciting new wave of diverse wine flavours.

The fox grape's well-known fruit are edible cooked or raw, while its young leaves must be eaten cooked. An edible oil can

be made from the seeds. A fox-grape treat from the North American Cherokee and Choctaw peoples, grape dumplings or *panki' alhfola* in the Chickasaw language, is made by forming a dough from corn (gluten-free) or wheat flour, baking powder, grape juice, sugar, and oil or shortening, and dropping small pieces into a simmering pan of grape juice. The fox grape's aromatic, sweet, musky, earthy flavour makes it great for jellies, jams, juices, ice creams and pie fillings. The slightly acidic young leaves are a tasty vegetable once cooked, or can be used as wrappers for baked foods.

Yellowhorn

Xanthoceras sorbifolium (Sapindaceae)

Yellowhorn is considered a relict tree, the only species of the genus *Xanthoceras*, which – for now – is little known outside its native range. There it has long been treasured for its medicinal and edible use, not to mention its beauty and resilience in the face of adversity. It was recorded in a Chinese *materia medica* in 1406 CE under the name *Wen Guan Hua*, and it is in China today, more than 600 years later, that researchers, breeders and farmers are coming together to understand and maximize the potential of this exceptional small deciduous tree. Ancient wisdom meets modern science to drive demand from the food, pharmaceutical, cosmetic, biofuel and greening industries. A major barrier to greater commercialization is self-incompatibility, an evolutionary trait to prevent inbreeding that, in isolated populations lacking diversity, has the unwelcome – albeit natural – outcome of poor fruit yield. In the case of yellowhorn it is doubly challenging, since both male and bisexual flowers occur on the same plant, which are typically propagated clonally from local trees. In 2017 scientists identified six genetic hotspots, the diversity of which is being introduced into plantations to increase productivity.

A member of the soapberry family, which gives us such beauties as buckeye, horse chestnut and maple, yellowhorn does not disappoint. In the late spring branches are laden with white flowers, each centred yellow, ageing to carmine red.

ALSO KNOWN AS
Shiny leaf yellowhorn, goldenhorn, Chinese flowering chestnut

NATIVE RANGE
China, Mongolia and Korea

NATURALIZED IN
Uzbekistan

GROWING CONDITIONS
Rocky slopes, hills and mountainsides in full sun on a range of dry acid to alkaline soils, including those of low fertility. Dislikes wet conditions.

WHERE TO FIND
The kernels and young leaves are available within its growing regions, while the oil can be bought from Chinese online retailers.

HOW TO EAT
Eat the peeled kernels as they are, or roasted or boiled. They are also the source of a healthy cooking oil that is rich in unsaturated fatty acids.

continues

The undersides of the petals have horn-like growths, hence the common name.

Yellowhorn is considered one of the most promising agroforestry subjects, and plantations have been established in northern China to combat desertification, since this tree is not only resistant to drought, wind and sand, but also hardy to at least -25°C (-13°F). Having oil-rich seeds, it offers interesting industrial possibilities for biofuel and bio-based chemicals, as well as for the regeneration of barren landscapes. That makes it an exciting cash and food crop for farmers on marginal land.

The young leaves and kernels can be eaten if they are cooked, and the seeds render a healthy oil, rich in unsaturated fatty acids. In countries where it is grown, the focus so far is mostly on the oil, but the peeled kernels are also eaten as they come, or roasted or boiled. Having a slightly waxy texture and a flavour reminiscent of cashews, they can be ground into a gluten-free flour. The young leaves and flowers, meanwhile, are usually eaten boiled.

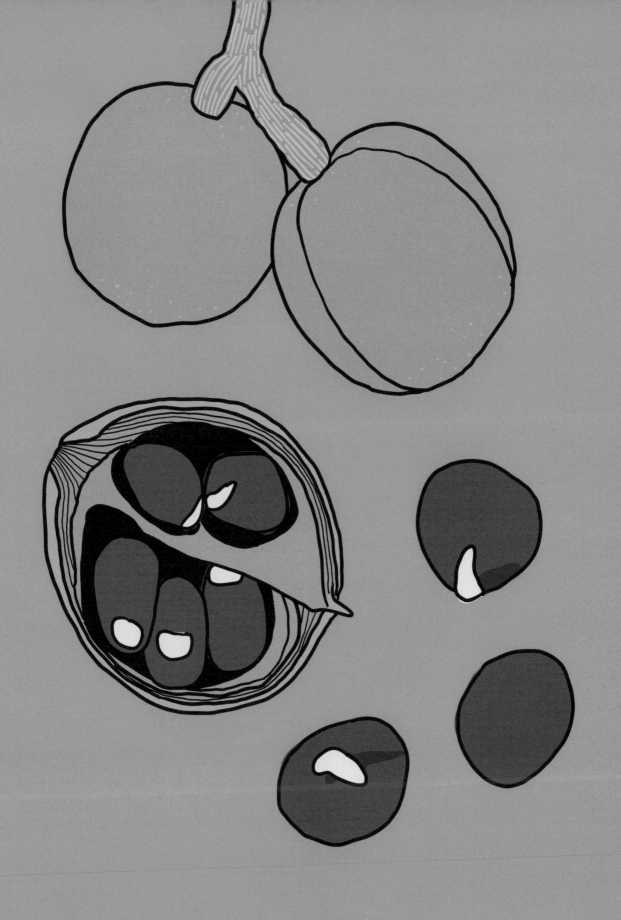

1

Sanshō

Zanthoxylum piperitum (Rutaceae)

Plant explorer, gardener or chef: many have been cajoled into chewing the tiny fruit of a *Zanthoxylum* species in what one might consider a rite of passage. Given that a handful of the 250 or so species are sold as Szechuan pepper, the act of eating one for the first time straight from the shrub seems daring. A numbing sensation is experienced on the tongue and/or in the mouth, varying in intensity according to species and ripeness. For these fruit are, typically, covered in minute oil-filled warts containing the compound hydroxy-alpha-sanshool, which stimulates receptors, producing a similar effect to that of local anaesthetic. If it is immediately followed by a sip of water, many experience the sensation of a mild electric shock to the tongue, a popular party trick shared by those in the know. *Z. armatum*, a native of a region from the Indian subcontinent to temperate East Asia, is one of the main sources of Szechuan pepper, and also enjoyed within the popular Chinese five-spice mix.

Although it is often hidden under the ambiguous Szechuan label, *Z. piperitum*, known as sanshō, is gaining popularity beyond its home. Being an extremely sought-after spice crop that thrives on a host of soils through frost and heat, all the while being tolerant of shade, makes it a great shrub for a medium layer in restorative agroforestry tree systems.

The fruit, young leaves and shoots of sanshō are eaten cooked or raw. A curious Japanese confectionary, *kirisanshō*, is a sweet *mochi* (rice cake) flavoured with ground sanshō. The fruit has a strong peppery, citrus flavour (the genus is in fact related to citrus), and it is the standard spice for the Japanese freshwater eel dish *unagi-kabayaki*, as well as a host of other dishes. Most often the ripe red fruit **(1)** is dried, freed of its flavour-diluting seed, and ground into a powder. But the fresh green fruit **(2)**, often (erroneously) called 'berries', can also be eaten pickled or used to infuse oils, sauces and even liqueur. The young leaves and shoots are used to garnish fish, in soups, and for sauces and pesto.

ALSO KNOWN AS
Japanese pepper, Japanese prickly ash, kona-zanshō, chopi, toothache tree

NATIVE RANGE
Eastern Himalaya, Japan, Korea

GROWING CONDITIONS
A large shrub hardy to at least -20°C (-4°F) on a range of moist, free-draining, neutral or lightly acid to lightly alkaline soils from sand to heavy clay.

WHERE TO FIND
Fresh parts can be found at markets in Japan, China and Korea; the dried spice is available from speciality food stores worldwide.

HOW TO EAT
Use as a peppery, citrusy spice for soups, sauces and fish dishes, and even to flavour sweet *mochi*.

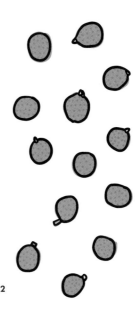

2

Jujube

Ziziphus jujuba (Rhamnaceae)

From a back catalogue of ancient plant-based medicines, the genus *Ziziphus*, containing about seventy-six recognized species, has in the early twenty-first century been subject to a flurry of scientific study, much of which suggests that it is the latest superfood. Such an accolade must amuse people throughout tropical, subtropical and warm temperate regions of the world to which these species are native, as science concurs with generations of accumulated wisdom. For thousands of years the fruit of this modest shrub or medium-sized tree has been used to treat a veritable A–Z of ailments. The plant is armed (some species more than others) with sharp spines to deter grazing herbivores and protect the unassuming yellow flowers that precede the olive-shaped orange-red fruit that, in some species, are deliciously sweet.

One such species is *Z. jujuba*, commonly known as jujube, of which there are about 400 cultivars developed for taste, size and yield of fruit. Not surprisingly, spineless selections are preferred by farmers. It is native to Korea as well as to China, where, in Henan province, charred pits of jujube unearthed by archaeologists indicate its foraging and domestication in Neolithic times, more than 7,000 years ago. Literary references chart jujube's popularity in its homelands and, via ancient trade routes, far beyond, including such warm temperate climates as Italy and parts of France. China's oldest surviving poetry, the seventh-

century BCE *Shih-ching* (Book of Odes), records 'Jujube fruit picked in August and rice harvested in October'. Jujube has long ranked among China's most important fruit crops, and in the past production was subject to specific taxes that were closely monitored by officials.

Simultaneously resistant to heat, drought and cold, and all the while growing on everything from nutritionally poor, exposed cliffs to saline plains, the jujube is a true whizzkid among fruit trees. Add to that its fast growth, natural tendency to form thickets and good response to pruning, and it becomes the perfect edible hedge or windbreak.

The fruit is high in vitamin C and can be eaten raw or cooked. The fresh fruit has a texture like that of an apple, and a flavour to match, with hints of date. It can be dried, boiled, stewed, baked or even candied and used for everything from jellies, cakes and puddings to soups. In Korea a healthy tea, *daechu-saenggangcha*, is made by simmering dried jujube fruit with ginger for a couple of hours before straining the liquid.

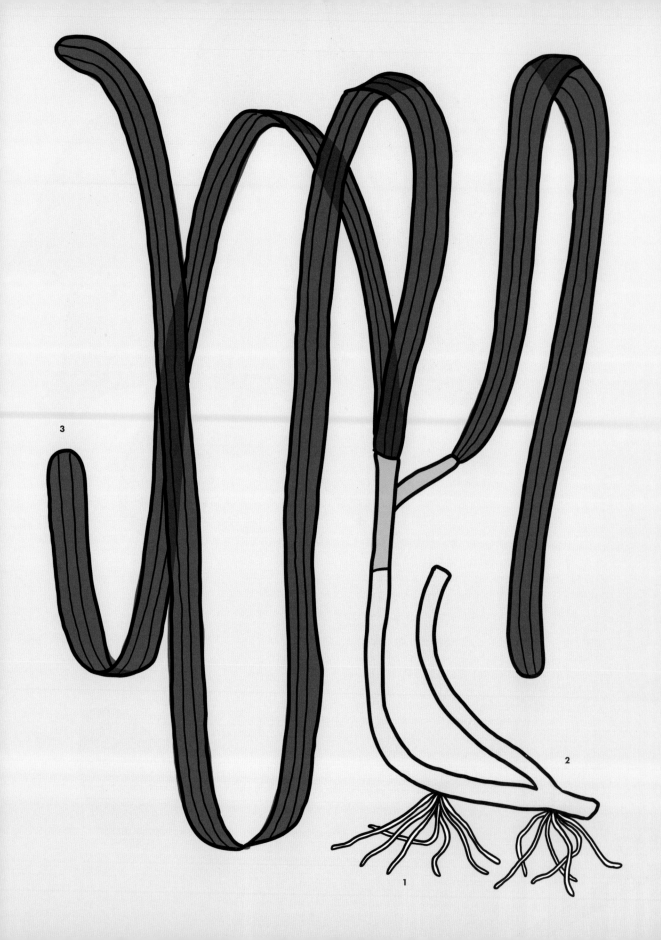

Marine Rice

Zostera marina (Zosteraceae)

Growing along coasts of every continent except Antarctica, seagrasses form vast meadows that have highly productive ecosystems as important as those of coral reefs and forests. These lush meadows in shallow salty waters provide shelter and food for marine life, mitigate against coastal erosion and draw down carbon dioxide up to thirty-five times faster than tropical rainforests. Recent studies suggest that they also play a role in cleaning the ocean of plastic waste, which is captured among the foliage and incorporated into natural fibre bundles called 'Neptune balls' that, once beached, can be removed. Seagrasses are often assumed to be seaweeds, but in fact they have roots **(1)**, stems **(2)**, leaves **(3)** and seed-producing flowers **(4)**, having migrated from land back to the ocean some 100 million years ago. This incredible feat of adaptation is now known to include a symbiotic relationship with nitrogen-fixing bacteria, in a fine example of convergent evolution, independently mirroring that of the legume family on land.

Of the four major groups and about seventy species of seagrass, *Zostera marina* is gaining gastronomic fame for its seed, which is often referred to as marine rice, although it looks more like amaranth grain. It is harvested in the spring and was historically a staple food for generations of Seri, the Indigenous hunter-gatherers who lived along the mainland coast of the Gulf of Mexico. Today its potential is championed by marine ecologists and chefs alike as a sustainable farmed crop of estuaries, but there is much work to be done to protect wild populations under

continues

continues

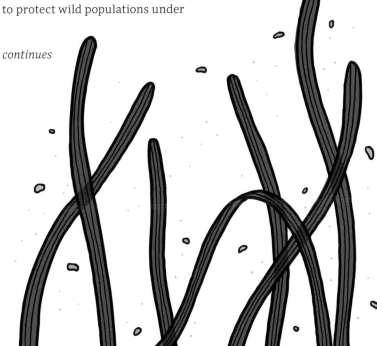

ALSO KNOWN AS
Da ye zao, eelgrass, grass wrack, sweet seagrass, meriajokas, zostère marine, Gewöhnliches Seegras, ålegras, herbe à bernaches

NATIVE RANGE
Throughout the temperate northern hemisphere of the Pacific and Atlantic

GROWING CONDITIONS
Intertidal and subtidal zones of shallow seas, where it grows in sandy, muddy and brackish coastal waters from tropics to Arctic at a depth of 0–5 m (0–16 ft).

WHERE TO FIND
Not yet available to buy, but can be foraged from the wild.

HOW TO EAT
Use the grains as you would rice. The fresh leaves can be added to salads or stir-fries.

threat from climate change, pollution and coastal development. Cultivation and, in some cases, reintroduction are increasing marine diversity and boosting local income through the harvest of marine rice, fish and crustaceans.

The leaves can be eaten raw or cooked, while the seed **(5)** is cooked or ground into flour. Having a similar texture and flavour to rice, with a slightly briny note, these grains can be used in much the same way as other varieties of rice. In a favourite recipe of the Seri people, *xnois kóinim*, marine rice is freed of its bran, roasted, then ground with cactus seeds into flour, before being cooked in water to produce gruel. The leaves, meanwhile, have a crisp texture and slight sweetness, making them a delicious addition to salads or stir-fries.

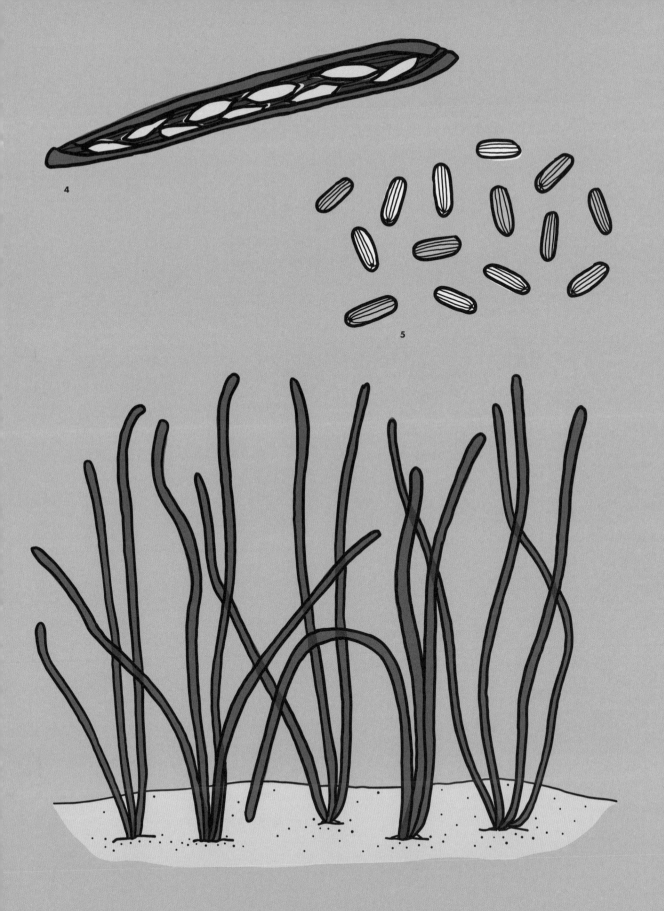

Glossary

ANGIOSPERMS
Flowering plants
(the majority of known
plant species).

ANNUAL
A plant that completes
its life cycle within
one growing season.

AQUACULTURE
The farming of aquatic
plants, either in a tank
or in open water.

AQUAPONICS
Using fish to enhance
aquatic plants
in a controlled
environment.

ARIL
An often edible
growth that covers the
outer part of a seed.

AXIL
The upper angle
between a stem or
branch and the branch
or trunk it grows from.

BULBIL
A bulb that forms
between a stem and
leaf or instead of
flowers on some plants.

CALYX
The sepals of a flower
(see sepal).

CLONAL PROPAGATION
Genetically identical
copies of a plant
produced by asexual
reproduction.

**CONVERGENT
EVOLUTION**
When species adapt
in similar ways in
response to similar
selective pressures.

COPPICING
A woodland
management
technique involving
felling trees to create
new shoots from
the stump.

CORM
A swollen
underground stem
that stores food for the
plant (see also tuber).

CULM
Above-ground stem
of a sedge or grass.

CULTIGEN
A plant genetically
altered by humans
that does not exist
in the wild.

DECIDUOUS
A tree or shrub
that loses its leaves
every year.

EUTROPHICATION
Nurient-induced
excessive plant and
algae growth in water.

EVERGREEN
A plant that keeps its
foliage over more than
one growing season.

**FIXATION (NITROGEN
AND CARBON)**
The process
of converting
atmospheric nitrogen
or inorganic carbon
into nutrients in
the soil.

HARDPAN
A hard layer of soil
that impairs drainage.

HYDROPONICS
The science of
growing plants
without using soil.

INFLORESCENCE
A cluster of flowers
on a branch or stem.

LEGUMES
Also known as pulses,
for example beans,
peanuts and lentils.

MICROGREENS
The seedlings of herbs
or vegetable plants.

OVARY
The female organ of a
flower, which matures
into a fruit.

PERENNIAL
A plant that lives
beyond two years.

PROPAGATION
The process of
growing new plants
from seeds or cuttings.

SEPAL
The outer parts of a
flower that enclose the
bud as it develops.

SILVOPASTURE
The practice of
integrating forage,
trees and animal
grazing to create a
mutually beneficial
system.

TUBER
An underground
storage organ in a
plant formed from
a stem or root – for
example a potato.

UMBELLIFER
Plants of the Apiaceae
family, characterized
by their umbrella-like
flowers.

Suppliers and Stockists

We have tried to ensure that the plants and produce featured in the book are readily available in their various regions and beyond. We hope that by using these plants more frequently in our food systems, we can help to ensure future food stability as well as increasing the variety of flavours on offer. If you live in an area teeming with vibrant local markets, international grocers, adventurous gardeners, foragers, growers, chefs or farmers, chances are that some of these plants can be tried and bought right around the corner from where you are. Exploring the options locally is an adventure just waiting to happen, with the potential for interesting new connections, inspirations, insights and the opportunity to support local economies.

If you want to discover even more, you can always turn to the internet. By shopping responsibly online – for example, by ordering in bulk together with friends and family to reduce emissions – you can also help to support vital initiatives and communities globally.

Below you will find a, by no means exhaustive, list of companies and organizations from around the world who are passionate about plant-based produce.

Produce

EUROPE

Gebana
www.gebana.com

Herbathek
www.herbathek.com

Lofoten Seaweed
lofotenseaweed.no

Tampopo Foods
www.tampopofoods.com

Shea WaLe
shop.sheabutter-ghana.de

VGCaviar
www.vgcaviar.com

Connemara Seaweed Company
www.connemaraseaweedcompany.ie

Col Spirit
www.col-spirit.com

Famberry
famberry2020.com.ua

25 Grams Coffee
www.25grams.coffee

Sanddorn Christine Berger
sanddorn-christine-berger.de

Jara
jara.earth

Jurassic Fruit
www.jurassicfruit.com

Spicemountain
www.spicemountain.co.uk

Dúlra
www.dulra.ie

Able & Cole
www.abelandcole.co.uk

THE AMERICAS

Kalustyan`s
foodsofnations.com

The Spice House
www.thespicehouse.com

Gulf of Maine
gulfofme.com

Regalis
www.regalisfoods.com

Pacific Botanicals
www.pacificbotanicals.com

Canopy Bridge
canopybridge.com

Earthy Delights
earthy.com

Red Fox Spices
redfoxspices.com

Finca Palugo
fincapalugo.com

Diaspora Co
www.diasporaco.com

Red de Guardianes de Semillas
redsemillas.org/english-seed-
guardians-network/

AFRICA

Essentially Natural
essentiallynatural.co.za

The Local Village
localvillage.africa

ASIA

Organic Fields
www.organicfields.com.my

Hiuchi Tonburi Production
Committee JA Akita (North)
ja-akitakita.jp/farming-and-life_
products-tonburi

Forest Post
forestpost.in

Kimura Food Co
www.kimura-food.co.jp

Minamiboso Online Market
shop.mboso-etoko.jp

OOO Farms
ooofarms.com

Banyan Roots
www.banyanroots.in

Arena Organica
www.arenaorganica.in

Arya Sanskriti
www.aryasanskriti.com

Aazol
aazol.in

Moringa What
www.moringawhat.com

OCEANIA

Footeside Farm
www.footesidefarm.com

Bush Food Shop
www.bushfoodshop.com.au

Plants and Seeds

EUROPE

Rein Saat
www.reinsaat.at

Arche Noah
shop.arche-noah.at

Rühlemann
www.kraeuter-und-duftpflanzen.de

Incredible Vegetables
www.incrediblevegetables.co.uk

Agroforestry Research Trust
www.agroforestry.co.uk

Kwekerij Bulk
kwekerijbulk.nl

Jurassic Plants
jurassicplants.co.uk

Franchi Seed
seedsofitaly.com

THE AMERICAS

Oikos Tree Crops
oikostreecrops.com

Trade Winds Fruit
www.tradewindsfruit.com

Trees of Joy
treesofjoy.com

AFRICA

Seeds & Plants
seedsandplants.co.za

Seeds for Africa
www.seedsforafrica.co.za

ASIA

Veliyath Gardens
veliyathgarden.com

OCEANIA

Daleys Fruit Tree Nursery
www.daleysfruit.com.au

Tucker Bush
tuckerbush.com.au

Foraging Location Guide

If you want to try foraging for plants from the book, the list below can be used to check what can be found growing in your area. Each plant column identifies the countries or regions in which plants are known to be native or have become naturalized. Following the simple rules from pages 54–55, the list is a great starting point for any foraging adventure, allowing you to meet the future stars of a resilient food system up close and personal. It is also a fantastic casting list if you want to check a plant's availability for a performance in your own garden. As always when foraging, do seek expert guidance if you're not familiar with a particular plant before picking it out in the wild for consumption.

PLANT	EUROPE	THE AMERICAS	AFRICA	ASIA	OCEANIA
Gurganyan (*Acacia colei*), p. 16				India	Western Australia
African baobab (*Adansonia digitata*), p. 18			Tropical and sub-tropical regions	Arabian Peninsula and much of Asia	
Grains of paradise (*Aframomum melegueta*), p. 20		French Guiana, Guyana, Trinidad and Tobago, Windward Islands	Western tropical Africa to Angola		
Winged kelp (*Alaria esculenta*), p. 22	Atlantic coast	North American Atlantic coast		Sea of Japan	
Hopniss (*Apios americana*), p. 24	France, Germany, Italy	Eastern North America		Japan, South Korea	
Great burdock (*Arctium lappa*), p. 28	Across Europe	Temperate North America		Temperate regions	
Breadfruit (*Artocarpus altilis*), p. 30		Tropical regions of Latin America and the Caribbean	Tropical regions	Tropical regions	Tropical regions
American pawpaw (*Asimina triloba*), p. 32		Southeastern Canada, central and eastern United States			
Mediterranean saltbush (*Atriplex halimus*), p. 34	Belgium, Macaronesia, Mediterranean, Netherlands, St Paul Island, United Kingdom		Northeastern tropical Africa	Arabian Peninsula, Iran, western Iraq	

PLANT	EUROPE	THE AMERICAS	AFRICA	ASIA	OCEANIA
Peach palm (*Bactris gasipaes*), p. 36		Tropical and subtropical Latin America and Caribbean			
Desert date (*Balanites aegyptiaca* var. *aegyptiaca*), p. 40			Much of Africa	Israel to Arabian Peninsula	
Vine spinach (*Basella alba*), p. 42		Belize, Brazil, Florida	Tropical and subtropical regions	Tropical and subtropical regions	
Kochia (*Bassia scoparia*), p. 44	Cool to warm temperate regions	Cool to warm temperate North America, Argentina	Algeria, Libya, Morocco, South Africa	Cool to warm temperate and subtropical regions	New Zealand
Wax gourd (*Benincasa hispida*), p. 46		The Caribbean, Venezuela		Tropical regions	Tropical regions
Palmyra palm (*Borassus flabellifer*), p. 48			Mauritania	Tropical regions	
Safflower (*Carthamus tinctorius*), p. 50	Across Europe	West Coast and temperate to dry North America, Mexico, much of South America, Cuba, El Salvador	North Africa, Mozambique, Zimbabwe	Across Asia	Across Oceania
Sea grapes (*Caulerpa lentillifera*), p. 52				Indo-Pacific coast	Indo-Pacific coast
Plumed cockscomb (*Celosia argentea*), p. 56	Albania, Bulgaria, Czech Republic, Italy, Romania, Slovakia	Florida	Seasonally dry tropical regions		Seasonally dry tropical regions
Carob (*Ceratonia siliqua*), p. 58	Mediterranean	Mexico, Peru	North Africa, seasonally dry tropical to subtropical regions	Much of the Middle East, the Caucasus, China, India, Pakistan	Australia
Irish moss (*Chondrus crispus*), p. 60	Atlantic coast	North American Atlantic coast			
Coffee cherry (*Coffea arabica* and *C. canephora*), p. 62		Tropical regions of Latin America from Mexico to Brazil	DRC, Ethiopia, Guinea-Bissau, Kenya, Malawi, Rwanda, Sudan	Bangladesh, China, Indonesia, Myanmar, Vietnam	Melanesia
Cornelian cherry (*Cornus mas*), p. 64	Northern and Continental western Europe east to Ukraine	Illinois, New York, Pennsylvania		The Caucasus, Lebanon, Russia, Syria, Turkey	
Tiger nut (*Cyperus esculentus*), p. 66	Across Europe	Across the Americas	Across Africa	Much of the Middle East, Afghanistan, Cambodia, China, the Caucasus, India, Pakistan, Indonesia, Vietnam	Across Oceania

PLANT	EUROPE	THE AMERICAS	AFRICA	ASIA	OCEANIA
Fonio millet (*Digitaria exilis*), p. 68		Dominican Republic, Haiti	Western tropical Africa to Cameroon		
Vegetable fern (*Diplazium esculentum*), p. 72		Florida, Hawaii	South Africa	East, Southeast and South Asia	Australia, New Zealand, Papua New Guinea
Mountain spinach (*Elatostema involucratum*), p. 76				China, Japan, Korea	
Enset (*Ensete ventricosum*), p. 78		Juan Fernández Islands	Western, southwestern and southern Africa, Gulf of Guinea islands	Indonesia	
Culantro (*Eryngium foetidum*), p. 80		Mexico to Brazil, subtropical regions of North America	Tropical regions	Southeast Asia	Pacific Islands
Bolivian fuchsia (*Fuchsia boliviana*), p. 82	Spain, Réunion	California, Hawaii, Jamaica, Mexico, much of Central and South America		Indonesia	New Zealand
Roselle (*Hibiscus sabdariffa*), p. 84		Belize, Brazil, Colombia, Cuba, El Salvador, Guatemala, Mexico, Peru, Venezuela	West, central to southern Africa, Egypt	Iraq, South and Southeast Asia	
Sea buckthorn (*Hippophae rhamnoides*), p. 88	Across Europe	Canada		Russia to western Himalaya	
Yuki urui (*Hosta*), p. 90	Bulgaria, Czech Republic, Romania, Slovakia	Eastern United States		China, Japan, Korea, Uzbekistan	
Sweet potato leaves (*Ipomoea batatas*), p. 92	Greece, Portugal, Spain	Latin America and Caribbean, subtropical and warm temperate regions of North America	Across Africa	South and Southeast Asia, the Caucasus, Turkmenistan, Tajikistan, Kyrgyzstan	Across Oceania
Sweet bush mango (*Irvingia gabonensis*), p. 94			Central Africa	India	
Indian butter tree (*Madhuca longiflora* var. *longiflora* and *Madhuca longifolia* var. *latifolia*), p. 96				Bangladesh, India, Nepal, Sri Lanka,	
Acerola cherry (*Malpighia emarginata*), p. 98		Mexico to Peru, islands of the Caribbean Sea			New Caledonia
Sapodilla (*Manilkara zapota*), p. 100		Florida, Mexico to Colombia, islands of the Caribbean Sea		Bangladesh	

PLANT	EUROPE	THE AMERICAS	AFRICA	ASIA	OCEANIA
Spanish lime (*Melicoccus bijugatus*), p. 104		Florida, Colombia, Costa Rica, El Salvador, islands of the Caribbean Sea, Venezuela			
Oysterleaf (*Mertensia maritima*), p. 106	Temperate to polar regions	Temperate to polar regions of North America		Temperate to polar regions	
Murnong (*Microseris walteri*), p. 108					Australia
Moringa (*Moringa oleifera*), p. 112		Arizona, California, Central America, Florida, islands of the Caribbean Sea, Venezuela	West, Central Africa to Angola, Libya, Madagascar	South and Southeast Asia	Australia
Red banana (*Musa acuminata*), p. 118	Spain	Costa Rica, Ecuador, Florida, Juan Fernández Islands, Trinidad and Tobago	Senegal, Tanzania	South and southeast Asia, Turkey	Caroline Islands, Fiji, French Polynesia, Nauru, Niue, Samoa, Tonga
Yangmei (*Myrica rubra*), p. 122				China, Japan, Korea, Philippines	Marianas islands
Nutmeg (*Myristica fragrans*), p. 124	Réunion		Comoros, Gulf of Guinea islands, Mauritius	Bangladesh, China, India, Indonesia, Laos, Philippines, Thailand, Vietnam	
Prickly pear (*Opuntia ficus-indica*), p. 126	Mediterranean	Arizona, California, Florida, New Mexico	Dry tropical and subtropical regions	Dry tropical and subtropical regions of South and Southeast Asia	Dry tropical and subtropical regions of Australia
African rice (*Oryza glaberrima*), p. 130		Brazil, Suriname	Benin, Burkina, Cameroon, Chad, Gambia, Guinea, Guinea-Bissau, Ivory Coast, Mali, Niger, Senegal, Togo	China	
Safou (*Pachylobus edulis*), p. 134			Angola, Cameroon, Central African Republic, Congo, Equatorial Guinea, Gabon, Gulf of Guinea islands, Nigeria, Zambia		
Jicama (*Pachyrhizus erosus*), p. 136		Brazil, Central America, islands of the Caribbean Sea, Mexico, Venezuela	Cameroon, Gabon, Madagascar, Tanzania	South and Southeast Asia	Australia, Papua New Guinea
Henon bamboo (*Phyllostachys nigra var. henonis*), p. 140		Hawaii		China, Japan, Korea, Philippines, Vietnam	New Zealand

PLANT	EUROPE	THE AMERICAS	AFRICA	ASIA	OCEANIA
Tomatillo (*Physalis philadelphica*), p. 142	Belgium, Greece, Portugal, Spain and much of eastern and southeastern Europe	Arizona and eastern United States, Central America, Cuba, Haiti, Mexico	Angola, Kenya, Morocco, South Africa, Sudan, Zambia, Zimbabwe	China, Russia, Turkey	Australia
Vallonea oak (*Quercus ithaburensis* subsp. *macrolepis*), p. 144	Greece, Italy and southeastern Europe			Lebanon, Syria, Turkey	
Black radish (*Raphanus raphanistrum* subsp. *sativus* (syn. *Raphanus sativus* var. *niger*)), p. 148	France, Greece, Italy, Portugal, Spain and southeastern Europe	North America, much of Central and South America, Cuba, Dominican Republic, Haiti	Angola, Eritrea, Ethiopia, Kenya, North Africa, South Africa, Sudan, Tanzania, Zimbabwe	Across Asia	Australia
Cosconilla (*Reichardia picroides*), p. 150	Mediterranean	Hawaii	North Africa	Syria, Turkey, UAE	Australia
Loquat (*Rhaphiolepis bibas*), p. 152	France, Greece, Italy, Portugal, Spain	Subtropical and warm temperate regions of North America, Mexico to Brazil	Kenya, South Africa	Much of East Asia, Afghanistan, the Caucasus, India, the Middle East, Pakistan, Thailand, Uzbekistan, Vietnam	Australia, New Zealand
Marsh samphire (*Salicornia europaea*), p. 154	Northern and central Europe				
Marula (*Sclerocarya birrea*), p. 158			West, central to southern Africa, Madagascar		
Heirloom potato varieties (*Solanum tuberosum*), p. 160	Belgium, France, Ireland, United Kingdom	Hawaii, eastern United States, much of South America, Dominican Republic, Haiti	DRC	Bangladesh, India, Russia, Tajikistan, Uzbekistan, Vietnam	
Tamarind (*Tamarindus indica*), p. 162		Much of Central and South America, Florida, islands of the Caribbean Sea, Mexico, Texas	West, central to southern Africa, Comoros, Egypt, Libya, Madagascar	Arabian Peninsula, South and Southeast Asia	Australia, Melanesia
Dandelion (*Taraxacum officinale*), p. 164	Across Europe	Across North America and South America, except Amazon basin	Cameroon, DRC, Madagascar, Morocco, Namibia, South Africa, Zimbabwe	Much of East Asia, India, Indonesia, Malaysia, Philippines	Australia, New Zealand
Prekese (*Tetrapleura tetraptera*), p. 166			Much of West and Central Africa, south to Angola		
Chinese toon (*Toona sinensis*), p. 168		Maryland	Tanzania, Uganda	Much of East and Southeast Asia, Afghanistan, Nepal, Pakistan, Sri Lanka, Sumatra	

PLANT	EUROPE	THE AMERICAS	AFRICA	ASIA	OCEANIA
Water caltrop (*Trapa natans*), p. 174	Much of central, eastern and southeastern Europe	East coast of Canada and United States	Central to southern Africa, Algeria, Burkina Faso, Tunesia	Across Asia	
Moth bean (*Vigna aconitifolia*), p. 176			Eritrea	Bangladesh, China, India, Myanmar, Pakistan, Sri Lanka, Yemen	
Bambara groundnut (*Vigna subterranea*), p. 178		Dominican Republic	Much of West and Central Africa, south to Zambia and Eswatini, Madagascar, Tanzania	India, Indonesia	Papua New Guinea
Fox grape (*Vitis labrusca*), p. 180	Albania, Austria, France, Greece, Hungary, Italy, Portugal, Spain, Ukraine	Much of the eastern United States		Russia, Tajikistan, Turkey, Turkmenistan, Uzbekistan, Vietnam	
Yellowhorn (*Xanthoceras sorbifolium*), p. 182				China, Korea, Mongolia, Uzbekistan	
Sanshō (*Zanthoxylum piperitum*), p. 186				China, Japan, Korea,	
Jujube (*Ziziphus jujuba*), p. 188	Southeastern Europe, France, Mediterranean, Spain	Alabama, Arizona, California, Cuba, Dominican Republic, Florida, Honduras, Jamaica, Louisiana, Texas, Utah, Venezuela	Algeria, Burkina Faso, Cameroon, Morocco, Tunisia, Libya	Much of the Middle East and Central Asia, Afghanistan, China, Georgia, India, Japan, Korea, Laos, Mongolia, Pakistan	
Marine rice (*Zostera marina*), p. 190	Temperate Atlantic and Mediterranean coasts	Temperate Atlantic coast of North America, Belize, Mexico	North African Atlantic and Mediterranean coasts	Temperate Pacific coast	

Biographies

KEVIN HOBBS is a plantsman, horticulturist and grower with over thirty-five years' experience. He has one foot planted in the botanical world, the other in commercial production and, for the last couple of decades, a mind increasingly focused on sustainability and countering climate change.

Working with likeminded friends and colleagues globally, he enjoys sharing knowledge and introducing new ornamental and edible plants to the market through his role as New Product Director at Whetman Plants International. A passionate advocate of all things green and growing, shared through talks, social media and publications, which include the book *The Story of Trees* (Laurence King, 2020). Kevin can be found at *@florafanatic* on Instagram.

ARTUR CISAR-ERLACH is an author, ecologist and food communications expert whose work spans the fields of food, woodland advocacy and videography.

He received his graduate degree in ecology at the University of Vienna and his postgraduate degree in Food Culture and Communications at the University of Gastronomic Sciences in Pollenzo, Italy.

Fascinated by the power of food he explores its immense potential for solving some of society's biggest contemporary challenges. A passion that he shares through workshops, talks and publications, such as his award-winning book, *The Flavor of Wood* (Abrams, 2019). Artur can be found at *@artur_cisar_erlach* on Instagram, *@ArturCisarErlach* on YouTube and at *arturcisar-erlach.com*.

KATIE KULLA is an illustrator and author based in the Pacific Northwest, where she lives and farms with her family. Her work focuses on nature, farming and family, and has appeared in *Taproot*, *Growing for Market*, *Farmer-ish*, *GreenPrints* and *Geez* magazines. This is her first book project. Katie can be found at *KatieKulla.com* and on Instagram: *@katiekulla*.

Acknowledgments

KEVIN HOBBS: To my family for their support, encouragement and endless patience as I burn the candle at both ends! Thank you, Artur, Katie and the Thames & Hudson team for joining me on this journey into the world's botanical larder. To the unending work and dedication of international collaborative programmes such as Plants of the World Online and International Union for Conservation of Nature and to all my plant friends far and wide, particularly plantsmen/botanists Mikinori Ogisu, James Armitage, Philippe Bonduel and John Grimshaw.

A quote of composer Sergei Rachmaninoff comes to mind, 'music is enough for a lifetime, but a lifetime is not enough for music'. A sentiment I share and apply to the world's wonderful, albeit vulnerable, diversity of plants, ferns, algae and fungi.

ARTUR CISAR-ERLACH: My deepest gratitude goes to my parents and partner whose unwavering support, advice and sheer endless patience makes projects like this book possible in the first place.

A big thank you to Kevin for bringing me on board with this one-of-a-kind project, what a fantastic adventure it has been! Thank you to Katie for bringing the stars of our book alive in such a vivid and colourful way, thank you to Rosie for shaping our dense thicket of a manuscript into a beautiful, tended garden and thank you to Lucas Dietrich, Fleur Jones and Helen Fanthorpe alongside the whole Thames & Hudson team for taking on and so elegantly guiding us through the maze of decisions, tasks and obstacles until publication.

Finally, a huge thank you goes to food friends all around the world whose insights, detective work and incredibly willingness to help made the seemingly impossible possible!

Our combined thanks to fellow plant and food enthusiasts goes to: John Fielding, Faten Zubair Filimban, Anna-Rose Ncube, Kumud Dadlani, Keith Kirsten, Felice Arena, Pei-Chen Lien, Cuauhtémoc Navarro, Rohit Jain, Naomi Beddoe, Gaurav Gurjar, Clarice Mojinum, Makiko Sato, Lukas Leitsberger, Udeshika Weerakkody, Nadeesha Lewke Bandara, Estefania Baldeon, Franklin Fok Lok, Petra Illig, Joshua Obaga, Laetitia Moucheboeuf, Francesca Grazioli, Marc-Henri Doyon, Maria L. Cobo, Charles Valin, Anel van der Merwe and Ross Cameron.

KATIE KULLA: Thank you to Fleur Jones, Ashlea O'Neill, Kevin Hobbs and Artur Cisar-Erlach for being an amazing team to work with on this book. And, to my family, for your cheerleading and support.

Index

FRONT COVER, LEFT TO RIGHT: moringa seeds, vine spinach and wax gourd flower; spine: grains of paradise; **BACK COVER, LEFT TO RIGHT:** tamarind seeds, red banana leaf and Irish moss.

First published in the United Kingdom in 2023 by
Thames & Hudson Ltd, 181A High Holborn, London WC1V 7QX

First published in the United States of America in 2023 by
Thames & Hudson Inc., 500 Fifth Avenue, New York, New York 10110

Edible: 70 Sustainable Plants That Are Changing How We Eat © 2023
Thames & Hudson Ltd, London

Text © 2023 Kevin Hobbs and Artur Cisar-Erlach
Illustrations by Katie Kulla
Designed by Ashlea O'Neill | Salt Camp Studio

British Library Cataloguing-in-Publication Data
A catalogue record for this book is available from the
British Library

Library of Congress Control Number 2023935983

ISBN 978-0-500-02561-1

Printed and bound in China by C&C Offset Printing Co. Ltd

Be the first to know about our new releases,
exclusive content and author events by visiting
thamesandhudson.com
thamesandhudsonusa.com
thamesandhudson.com.au